American Golf in the Great Depression

The Pros Take to the Grapefruit Circuit

KEVIN KENNY

Foreword by MARTY KAVANAUGH

McFarland & Company, Inc., Publishers

Jefferson, North Carolina

ISBN 978-0-7864-7812-5 (softcover : acid free paper) ∞
ISBN 978-1-4766-1501-1 (ebook)

LIBRARY OF CONGRESS CATALOGUING DATA ARE AVAILABLE

BRITISH LIBRARY CATALOGUING DATA ARE AVAILABLE

On the cover: *inset:* "Lord" Byron Nelson in action at the 1935 North
and South in Pinehurst (Tufts Archives, Pinehurst); *bottom:* 7th hole,
Pebble Beach Golf Course, Del Monte, CA (Library of Congress)

Printed in the United States of America

*McFarland & Company, Inc., Publishers
Box 611, Jefferson, North Carolina 28640
www.mcfarlandpub.com*

American Golf in
the Great Depression

For my father, E.J. Kenny,
who introduced me to the wonderful
game of golf many years ago

Contents

Acknowledgments

There are a number of people to whom I am deeply indebted in regard to the completion of this book. In terms of my research, the staff at the USGA Library in Far Hills, New Jersey, were very helpful, especially Nicole Ciaramella in the photographic archives, with her guidance and limitless patience. I am grateful also to all the team at the PGA Museum of Golf in Port St. Lucie, Florida. A special thank you goes to Audrey Moriarty and Kay Lund at the Tufts Archive, Pinehurst, North Carolina, and to Maria Eipert at the Smithsonian Library, Washington, D.C. The British Newspaper Library in London also provided me with invaluable help researching numerous American titles, as did the staff at the University of Florida libraries.

I am deeply indebted to Marty Kavanaugh for writing the foreword for this book and for his encouragement from the start of this project. Special thanks also go to Beth Davis; Bill Quirin; Bill O'Keefe; Jennifer Vinnitti; Susan Wakefield; Judy Corcoran; Paul Daley; Mike Nix; Monique Sugimoto; Ellen Sieber; Penny Harris Healy; Gordon McInnes; General Mills, Inc.; Jason Cheong; Pam Whitenack; Randy Huber (a Hershey Country Club historian); Tom Creavy; Kent Ahlf; Monte McNew; Doug Dickey; Lawson Little III; and Tom Watson, who all helped me greatly in a variety of ways.

One of the joys of researching my topic was seeing the enthusiasm shown by a number of golf clubs. I extend my deepest appreciation to Deal CC; Medinah CC; Wilshire CC; the Craig Wood Golf Course; Salem CC; Glen Oak CC; Winged Foot; and Baltusrol.

Finally, but not least, my deepest thanks are due my family—Celia, Jo, Stephen, Heather and Matthew—for their unstinting support during the writing and completion of this book.

Foreword

by Marty Kavanaugh

As one studies the history of the Professional Golfers' Association of America it becomes very clear that the entire timeline on display at the PGA Museum of Golf in Port St. Lucie, Florida, could easily be consumed with the development of the Association from 1920 to 1940. While the Great Depression was in full swing during much of this time, so was the flowering of the PGA of America. In these "hard times," vestiges of the romantic Roaring '20s continued to drive the expansion of the game and the Association for years.

It is interesting to note that the birth of the PGA of America took place only three years after the historic victory of a young caddie, Francis Ouimet, in the U.S. Open at the Country Club, over Harry Vardon ("The Stylist") and the swashbuckling Ted Ray. The growth of the game in the 10 years following 1913 was dramatic and could arguably have been the direct cause of the necessity to form a fraternity of professional golfers, to service the burgeoning masses desiring to play the game.

However, "who" Francis Ouimet motivated to become "the professionals" of the game proved to be the seed from which grew the largest working sports organization in the world. Ouimet inspired many young caddies of the day, showing them that they could do it, too! They could rise above, they could be heroes, and they did not have to be relegated to the status of "poor immigrant" by upper echelons of society for the rest of their lives.

The 1920s and 1930s were a magnificent time in the history of the Association, and the programs developed by the Association during this time are too staggering to cover in their entirety here. Nevertheless, a few are important to mention: an Employment Bureau; a Professional Education Department; a Golf Course Services Department headed by A.W. Tillinghast; a Tournament Department to drive the idea of a "show window" for golf; and the concept of charitable giving, so that non-golfers suffering in our country could share in the fruits of the game.

In this book, Kevin Kenny takes one slice of the PGA, the most exciting slice, the beginning and growth of the PGA's Tour, and literally transports us back in time to the people, the places, the events and the excitement of those difficult but glorious days and makes anyone remotely interested in the history of the game of golf dream of being there. Golf is a game that historically has never forgotten its heroes; Kevin Kenny, through these beautiful accounts, proves this to be true.

As a second-generation PGA golf professional, growing up with and caddying for a father who was a fine player competing in the Senior PGA Championship at Dunedin Country Club in Clearwater, Florida, against the likes of Sam Snead, Jimmy Demaret and Paul Runyan, I will forever remember my first trip to the Seniors' with my dad. Passing behind the 10th tee at Dunedin, my dad said, "Stop; watch. That is Jimmy Demaret." I will never forget that tee shot, the first I had ever seen disappear into the horizon. At that moment I decided I wanted to be just like these men: I wanted to be a golf professional. So from Jimmy Demaret to just another caddie, from Francis Ouimet to all of us, the dream continues. I therefore will attest to the fact that you, too, will be transported back there when you read this book. And perhaps you will even wish that you could have been so unfortunate as to be a caddie at that time, and maybe, just maybe...

Kevin, thanks for the memories and for this engaging stroll through our history.

After a 30-year career, retiring as manager of golf for the Hamilton County Park District in Cincinnati, Marty Kavanaugh joined the PGA of America staff in 1994, eventually overseeing many departments of the PGA. In 2005, he was inducted into the PGA of America's Golf Professional Hall of Fame.

Preface

I once taught American history in an academic setting and found there is an abundance of literature on the Great Depression. However, as someone for whom golf's past has long been a passion, I came to believe that this era had not been given enough detailed attention by the game's eminent chroniclers. So I decided to fill a gap in the written history of the game and write about the Grapefruit Circuit—the name given to the tour in recognition of the fact that many of the tournaments were played in Florida and California. This is not to suggest that the Depression years have been entirely neglected. For example, Herbert Warren Wind deals with them in his magisterial *The Story of American Golf.* In addition, Al Barkow's *Golf's Golden Grind, Gettin' to the Dance Floor,* and *The Golden Era of Golf* vividly bring to life some of the characters who dominated and influenced the game during the Depression years. Furthermore, the more recent *American Triumvirate* by James Dodson sees the author craft a beautiful account of the lives of three of the "greats" of American golf: Ben Hogan, Byron Nelson, and Sam Snead. Dodson devotes a good deal of time to the Depression years when all three future champions embarked on their professional careers.

Still, it is my belief that this rich period in American golf history has been sandwiched in between the golden 1920s, when Jones, Hagen and Sarazen ruled, and the 1940s and 1950s, when Hogan, Nelson and Snead dominated. When I look at the Grapefruit Circuit in detail, I start with 1931 even though the Great Depression began in 1929. There is a golfing reason for this: I felt it was better to look at the tour after Bobby Jones retired. This is not in any way meant to be disrespectful to Jones and his phenomenal accomplishments. However, in 1929 and 1930, Jones dominated the game (and the golfing media) to such an extent that even

3

though he was an amateur, it would have been difficult to avoid retelling his achievements, notably in his Grand Slam year of 1930. The aim of the book is to provide an account of many of the players who may not be as well known as those who remain household names to this day, such as Sarazen, Nelson, and Snead, all of whom feature significantly in my book. But there were other wonderful golfers whose records speak for themselves. I am thinking here of players such as Ralph Guldahl, Denny Shute, Henry Picard, and many, many more. My book also covers life on tour, sponsors and prize money levels, and the colorful politics of the game. Furthermore, it sets all of this against the background of the immense hardship endured by the United States during the period. The early chapters of the book look first at the "Roaring 1920s" and then at how the game in general was affected by the Great Depression. This background, I believe, is important in providing a fuller understanding of how things changed both for the game itself and for the professional golfer during the Depression years.

Since I am based in Ireland but writing on an American topic, some long journeys were necessary. Over a six-year period, my research took me to New Jersey to visit golf libraries and the headquarters of the USGA, and to Florida, home of the PGA. I also made the shorter trip to the British Newspaper Library in London where many American newspapers are held. I was fortunate to make many online connections with other sources of invaluable information such as Tufts Archives in Pinehurst, North Carolina; Golf Canada; the LA84 Foundation; and many golf clubs the world over. I like to think that, combined, these resources have helped me write a book that does justice to those individuals who contributed so much to professional golf during this dark period in American history.

Introduction

"But when I think of the twenties, I think of Florida.... It was Hollywood enlarged and blurred."[1]—Gene Sarazen

For much of the 1920s it seemed that America was experiencing a golden age. It was the age of glamour, F. Scott Fitzgerald, Jay Gatsby, and jazz. And it was also the era of Prohibition, which proved only a minor inconvenience for those who knew where to "get the real stuff." There were many in this category.

The 1920s (despite a slump in its first year) was also an era of almost full employment and by extension of great economic prosperity. Nowhere was this more evident than in the arrival of the affordable Ford motor car. In 1908, when the Model T (or "Tin Lizzie") was produced, it cost $850. However, with the advent of Henry Ford's standardized mass production techniques, the same car was down to $290 by 1924. Unsurprisingly, the number of registered cars rose from 8 million in 1920 to 23 million in 1929.[2] Many of these were bought on credit, but most important, a car was now accessible to the factory worker and lawyer alike. Ford's plan to "democratize the automobile" had come to pass.

This proliferation of automobiles helped to create an enormous growth in the number of motels and gas stations to cater to the needs of the new motorists. America was definitely on the move. The motor car, added to a rapidly rising stock market and a property boom, persuaded many Americans that anything was possible. Florida, in particular, symbolized this new age—it was a place new car owners could drive to and find a warm climate *and* a place where they could get rich by speculating on the seemingly endless rise in property prices. The consumer society had well and truly arrived and the American economic model was the envy of the world.

Sport also flourished and new heroes, such as Babe Ruth and Jack Dempsey, emerged. These men were not just stars in their respective sports of baseball and boxing but were also seen as celebrities, men who appeared on the social pages as well as in the sports columns. Jack Dempsey's love life, for example, was a boon to the newspapers, in particular the "will he or won't he marry Estelle Taylor" story. He did, in 1925. In a long "exclusive" the new Mrs. Dempsey told readers of their first kiss: "I'll never forget it even if I live to be a hundred."[3] Dempsey's manager, Jack Kearns, also let readers into Dempsey's private life with anecdotes of a trip to Europe. It seemed the French women were crazy for Jack while the women in London were charmed by his social graces. "While in London [Jack] proved as much at ease in a drawing room as he did in the ring."[4]

This decade also saw home-bred golf stars come to the fore. Ever since Francis Ouimet's victory in the 1913 U.S. Open and what is generally seen as the start of America's golfing hegemony, the game had increased significantly in popularity. When writing of this period, Richard Moss claimed that "America entered an era in which sport in general became more important, golf began to shed for good its upper-class image, and growing numbers of Americans made it part of their lives."[5] This was certainly the case as the number of country clubs increased, as did the amount of "pay to play" courses. Also, women's participation in golf, which had begun in the late 19th century, saw a significant increase as well.

As for the popularity of the top players, leading the way (and by some distance) was the incomparable amateur Bobby Jones, who captured the imagination of the sporting public as both boy and man. For many, Jones's success reinforced the image of golf as a still-amateur game. Ouimet was an amateur and remained so throughout his illustrious career, and there were other notable amateur golfers such as Jess Sweetser and George Von Elm. However, the 1920s was also the era when American-born professionals rose to the top. Traditionally it was argued that to be a "real" pro, one needed to be of British stock and preferably from Scotland. In that regard, the 1920s saw Scots-born Tommy Armour, Willie MacFarlane and Bobby Cruickshank make their mark on the game, as did Jim Barnes from Cornwall. But there is little doubt that the situation was changing, with home-bred American players starting to dominate the professional game.

Richard J. Moss argues that this decade saw the game become "Americanized" and went on to suggest that in the "late nineteenth century and earlier in the twentieth, the average American had tended to think of golf as somehow connected to Scotland and the English upper crust."[6] To connect with the wider public, the professional game needed home heroes—and their emergence is precisely what happened during the 1920s. Players such as Johnny Farrell and Leo Diegel made an impression with victories in the U.S. Open and PGA Championship, respectively. However, leading the beginning of dominance by home-bred American professionals were Walter Hagen and Gene Sarazen, who between them won 13 Majors during this decade and who would go on to become all-time legends of the game. Like Dempsey and Ruth, these men also became celebrities and were well placed to "cash in" on a society seemingly awash with money.

Gene Sarazen described the 1920s as "a nice slice of the century to be young in. The times were good, the parties were frequent, the girls were pretty, the drinks were long, the days were sunny, the nights were cool, and the stock market was strong as an ox."[7] As one of the star names in golf, Sarazen was well placed to take advantage both of the times and of golf's growing popularity. Apart from tournament prize money, top golfers could cash in by way of endorsements, exhibition matches at $300 per appearance and retainer fees from clubs which would benefit from their association with such famous names. Indeed, during these heady days, Sarazen recalled that he invariably read the financial columns before turning to the sports pages of his daily newspaper.[8] Sarazen's friend and rival Walter Hagen, who by virtue of his skill and personality had helped break down many of the game's social barriers, also enjoyed the 1920s and the celebrity status. "The Haig" especially enjoyed Florida.

Florida was a natural home for Hagen, who admitted he was attracted by the "sunshine, beautiful scenery, people with time on their hands for fun, and of course money."[9] Golf fit in neatly with Florida's landscape, and the state's warm winter climate made it a haven for the tourist whose business, according to *The American Golfer*, "is today one of the leading national industries. His account today runs into millions. An increasing number are willing to work through spring, summer and fall to get their vacation between January and late March ... and they can be certain of finding golf courses that make their trip worthwhile."[10] By the mid–1920s, it was estimated that were more than 100 courses in Florida.

As well as being ideal for the car owner, a further advantage the state had was a highly developed rail system on both its east and west coasts.

In Victorian Britain and Ireland, the growth of golf as a popular pastime was aided by strategically located rail links whereby tourists could literally step off the train and find themselves within easy walking distance of some of the most famous links courses. Not only this, but there were elegant hotels near at hand. Prestwick in Scotland and Newcastle on Ireland's northeast coast were two prime examples. Similarly, Florida's rail infrastructure, which made for easy access to the state's many hotel and leisure facilities, contributed to the growth of the game and of sports in general. As Paula Welch remarked of the decade, "A sporting atmosphere was created in the Sunshine state especially by those interested in promoting tourism."[11]

Arguably "those interested in promoting tourism" included journalists, who did the game and the state considerable service. For example, when writing of the state's west coast, noted writer O.B. Keeler lyrically described the golfing terrain as follows: "There is a springy turf under the feet and a cushioned green on which a well-hit pitch will bite firmly. There is a glistening white sand to punish the strayer from the straight and narrow path. And mostly there is the mellow thunder of surf in the ears and in the eyes those entrancing glimpses through the pines and moss of a deeper blue than ever yet was caught on canvas, etched with the white lines marching towards the beach. No wonder golf on the Florida West Coast is such a siren."[12] In addition to personally experiencing these golfing delights, the tourists who traveled south had the opportunity to see stars like Hagen play on the winter circuit.

The winter circuit formed the major part of what was then an emerging tour. Before this, professional "meetings," which began in the last decade of the 19th century, were often conducted on an *ad hoc* basis, with challenge matches occurring between local professionals such as the Fitzjohn brothers, Val and Ed. When Harry Vardon toured America in 1900, large crowds came to see the world's best player take on the home golfers in a series of exhibition matches. Typically, these matches might involve Vardon playing the best ball of two leading amateurs or professionals. On other occasions, he played a head-to-head match against a top pro such as George Low. The tour, which lasted almost a year, was sponsored by Spalding in an effort to promote the Vardon Flyer golf ball. Spalding got a good value for its money, as apart from attracting large numbers to his exhibition matches, Vardon took time out to win the United States Open Championship (U.S. Open). The Vardon Flyer, however, did not last long; it was soon surpassed by the rubber-cored Haskell ball, which even the great man himself adopted not long after his trip to America.

The U.S. Open was first held in 1895 and was played under the auspices of the United States Golf Association (USGA). Both professionals and amateurs competed for the trophy. In the tournament's early days, at least one newspaper felt obliged to explain to its readers how the professional differed from the amateur. Of the cash prizes on offer, it was recorded that "the money on offer shall be used by the amateur in the purchase of a plate, but by the professional as he sees fit."[13]

The "as he sees fit" comment could be interpreted as somewhat snobbish—and there may well have been more than a whiff of that at the time. Certainly the eminent golf writer and historian Al Barkow was in no doubt about this in his very thorough studies of the professional game. Barkow argued that at the start of the century, the growing golf resorts in the southern states promoted amateur tournaments with large advertisements in golf periodicals. However, he goes on to suggest that "it was mentioned, usually in a kind of stage whisper, that some professional matches would also be held. These were called opens, with a lower-case *o*, a conceit by which these professional-dominated events were put in the perspective of the time."[14]

Journalists were also known to adopt a rather lukewarm approach when reporting on the professionals. In 1902 the Marine and Field Club of New York announced that "arrangements have been completed for a professional golf match on the Marine and Field Club links on Saturday November 1."[15] The match was a foursome in which the previous year's National Open champions Willie Anderson and Gilbert Nichols were to play George Low and John A. Shippen. Again, the language is instructive, with the phrase "arrangements have been completed" being similar to that of a funeral notice. Certainly, there was a marked difference in style and emphasis between this era and the 1920s, when "Professionals Hit the Gold Trail" headlines frequented the newspapers.

It is fair to say, then, that while the professional game was growing in the early days of the century, it was not universally embraced. Similarly, there was little organization regarding the careers of the "play for pay" brigade or club professionals. Professional golf was run on largely regional lines, with no national body to administer and promote the game.

However, in January 1916, a lunch was held by Rodman Wanamaker at the Taplow Club, New York, which changed the face of professional golf in America. Wanamaker came from an extremely wealthy family that, among other interests, owned a group of prestigious department stores. Wanamaker was a man of many interests and used his wealth to sponsor trans–Atlantic aviation attempts as well as to start the renowned Milrose track and field meetings in 1908. However, perhaps his greatest sporting legacy was in professional golf. At the Taplow Club he invited a cross section of golf's great and good to the lunch, including 1913 National Open champion Francis Ouimet, course designer A.W. Tillinghast, and Walter Hagen. The aim was "to form an association of professional golfers of national scope."[16] The formation of this Professional Golfers' Association (PGA) was an important step in moving the professional game away from the amateur-centered image of golf, as the pros now had their own organization to direct policy.

Wanamaker also promised to donate prize money and a trophy for a tournament based loosely on the British *News of the World* match-play event. The tournament was held at the Siwanoy Club, New York, in October 1916 and the first winner in the 36-hole final was the English-born Jim Barnes, who defeated Scots-born Jock Hutchinson. *Sporting Life* described the championship as being "the finest exhibition of golf playing which has been seen in the United States since the beginning of the game in this country." It went on to note that "the gallery was never below 300 and on two occasions it rose to 3,000 showing the interest that the new tournament has aroused."[17] Barnes won $500, a diamond medal and a cup costing $1,000. The seeds of what became the third major had been sown, and to this day the winner of the Professional Golfers' Association Championship receives the Wanamaker trophy.

While Wanamaker and the others present at the lunch in January 1916 were very concerned at looking after club professionals, the decision to start a "PGA" championship was important, as it formalized the role that the new association would have in creating some form of structure regarding professional tournaments. It was significant, therefore, that when the PGA was officially founded a few months later, part of its mission was to "hold meetings and tournaments periodically for the encouragement of the younger members."[18] The language may appear slightly underwhelming. Perhaps because the PGA was formed during the war years, when there were more pressing matters to hand, the association did not envisage how important "meetings and tournaments" would become. But at least it was a start even if the PGA's formal involvement in the tour was some years away yet.

Typically, this new tour might begin on the West Coast in December and end in Arkansas in the spring. O.B. Keeler described the tour as an "odyssey" in which "the voyageurs are playing for a very great deal besides money. There was a fine adventure forward, not lacking in romance and abounding in sport."[19] While Keeler may have exercised some poetic

Rodman Wanamaker—aviation pioneer, business magnate, philanthropist and one of the founding fathers of the PGA (courtesy of the Mathers Museum of World Cultures, Indiana University).

license with his somewhat idealistic observations on the tough world of professional golf, his words seem to fit in with the spirit of the 1920s. And in a further nod to the plentiful mood of the 1920s, he went on to report how, on the way to tournaments, some of the more affluent players took drawing rooms on the trains.[20] Certainly times were better for the touring professionals. Indeed, in anticipation of the winter swing, David J. Walsh wrote of the riches available: "It has come to the season of the annual melon cutting when professionals are plied with fat contracts to represent clubs at popular resorts and tournaments are staged with cash prizes running into important thousands. Winter prerequisites have carried professional golf into the big money class and divided the field into two classes to wit: competitors and instructors."[21] There may have been a hint of hyperbole here but this was certainly a long way from the original aim of the PGA to periodically hold "meetings and tournaments to encourage younger members." Moreover, Walsh was certainly right about the "important thousands."

However, while the PGA was the professional's governing body, at this stage it remained largely focused on the club pros. It would not take charge of tournament matters until 1929, when journalist Hal Sharkey took on the unpaid job of arranging tournaments. Before that, tournaments were arranged on a hit-and-miss basis. According to Al Barkow, it was the wives of some leading professionals who were largely responsible for any advances the tour made in the mid–1920s. In particular, Estelle Armour, Josephine Espinosa and Nellie Cruickshank did the ground work. As Barkow recounts in *Golf's Golden Grind,* these three formidable women "spent many hours a day on telephones cajoling sponsors for more prize money, following up leads on potential sponsors and making travel and living arrangements for many of the pros."[22] Their work, and the growing attractiveness of professional golf for both fans and sponsors, was reflected in some substantial prize funds. For example, when Joe Turnesa won the Texas Open of 1925, the first prize was $1,500 and his victory was witnessed by a gallery of 5,000. The Los Angeles Open was one of the more prestigious tournaments and it too carried a substantial prize fund. For the inaugural event of 1926, there was a total purse of $10,000, with a first prize of $3,500 won by Harry Cooper. The Junior Chamber of Commerce underwrote the tournament.

But Florida was undoubtedly the center of golf at this time and the state hosted many important events and exhibition matches. It was also the place where there was clear evidence of the advances made by professional golf: a place where both newspapers and holiday-makers saw the top players as being both glamorous and newsworthy. Again, this was some distance from the snobbery which existed during the early days of professional golf in America. Florida was also the location of the famous 72-hole challenge match between Hagen and Bobby Jones in 1926, which Sir Walter won by 12 and 11. The victory was worth just short of $7,000 to Hagen. The state's oldest city, St. Augustine, also hosted a professional tournament and in many ways it highlighted the glamor of the 1920s. Apart from the professional stop, there were also amateur events where Jones and Ouimet competed and a five-day aquatic "carnival" which attracted women's Olympic swimmers and the celebrated Johnny Weismuller. The word "carnival" seemed to sum up both the events and the era.

There was also money to be made for land speculators in Florida. Renowned writer Grantland Rice compared the era to that of the California Gold Rush and claimed that "a plot of land that could have been bought for $10,000 two or three years ago is now selling for $75,000 or

$100,000."[23] Golf provided a natural link to the property boom, as many of the developments included newly built courses and relied heavily on a "name" player to attract investors. As the leading professional and undoubtedly the most glamorous, Hagen was the ideal man for this job. Indeed, in 1923, Hagen was named as the president of the Pasadena-on-the-Gulf course. For four months (December–March) he received an enormous $30,000 salary. His duties included arranging exhibitions and weekend tournaments in Pasadena and representing the course on the professional circuit.[24] Other top players who availed themselves of the "fat contracts" on offer from leading golf resorts included Gene Sarazen, Tommy Armour, Johnny Farrell, Leo Diegel, and Jim Barnes.

And it was not just the indigenous professionals who took advantage of Florida's boom. British professionals Abe Mitchell and George Duncan, the 1920 Open Champion, toured the state in 1925 and played in a number of tournaments and lucrative exhibitions. A slightly lesser-known British professional, Archie Compston, was another beneficiary of Florida's largesse. If Compston was not as successful as Hagen, he would soon become a Ryder Cup player and in 1928 would defeat Sir Walter 18 and 17 in a 72-hole challenge match in London. As well as being a fine player, Compston cut a handsome dashing figure. Certainly the millionaire property developer D.P. Davis was impressed with his credentials; he engaged Compston on a salary of $20,000 for a five-month contract to represent his luxury Davis Shores project in St. Augustine.[25] Davis also brought the French veteran and former Open Champion Arnaud Massy to Florida, where Massy teamed up with Compston in a number of exhibition matches to promote the St. Augustine venture. Davis Shores in total was a $50 million, 1,500-acre development, comprising apartments, yacht basins, and hotels, not to mention two championship golf courses. *The Miami News* heralded the venture as a place where "quick generous profits await investors,"[26] while the *St. Petersburg Times* predicted "another deluge of buying" and a "shower of checks for the developers."[27] Not only were Gene Sarazen and Leo Diegel attached to resorts in Florida, but these men also invested in real estate. It seemed as if nothing could go wrong—but it did.

In September 1926, the state was visited by a hurricane with devastating consequences for both life and the economy. Also, by the end of the year, the Florida property boom had collapsed. Hagen was not affected apart from the loss of salary, but along with thousands of others Sarazen and Diegel never saw a cent of profit from their investment. In March 1927, a receiver was appointed for the Davis Shores development.

While it was not immediately apparent, the Florida collapse was the precursor of the immense collective and individual hardship which followed a few years later. The "sunshine and bubbles"[28] of which Sarazen wrote were over and he admitted that golf was now his only resource. Along with most professionals he faced an uncertain future, as no one was sure how or if tournament professional golf would survive. Certainly the game had increased in popularity and was a sport with which more Americans connected. Also, as we have seen, America now had its own professional golfing heroes, not to mention an organization to run the pro game. To what extent it would endure, and survive the Great Depression which followed shortly after the Wall Street Crash of 1929, is the subject of this book.

CHAPTER 1

The Great Depression and Its Impact

"More important, a host of unemployed citizens face the grim problems of existence, and an equally great number toil with little return. Only a foolish optimist can deny the dark realities of the moment"—Franklin Roosevelt's inaugural address, 1933

While many historians can agree that the Great Depression began in 1930, in the aftermath of the 1929 Wall Street Crash, there has long been disagreement as to when it ended. To some, it took entry into World War II and the resulting surge in production to finally bring the U.S. economy back to rude health. What is not in doubt is the impact it had on life in America. The noted historian and Pulitzer Prize winner Carl Degler believed that the Great Depression rivalled the Civil War for its cataclysmic impact on American society and came close to "overturning the basic institutions of American life."[1] Much, but not all, of the hardship endured by millions during this decade would be eased by Franklin Delano Roosevelt's (FDR) New Deal.

The New Deal was a milestone in American history, as for the first time the federal government abandoned *laissez-faire* policies and actively took control of the economy. With unemployment running at over 25 percent in many areas, perhaps the most fundamental aim of the New Deal was to get Americans back to work. One of the numerous initiatives introduced by New Deal programmers was the Works Progress Administration (WPA) of 1935. This initiative was headed by FDR's advisor Harry L. Hopkins, who famously argued that "hunger is not debatable"[2] and whose brief was to "provide millions of jobs quickly."[3] Hopkins and his team certainly achieved their aims, often by recruiting unskilled labor, and by the time the WPA ceased operations during World War II, it had left a permanent legacy of bridges, roads, airports and schools.

Part of the hope Roosevelt sought to bring to Americans was a return to normality, and in this regard the WPA established cultural programmes designed to get writers, poets and artists back to work. For instance, the Federal Writers' Project at one period employed 6,000 writers from all levels, with unknown scribes working on the same payroll as John Steinbeck. Theater also benefited, with Orson Welles directing plays, and 40,000 people watching T.S. Eliot's *Murder in the Cathedral* at the Federal Theatre in New York. The top ticket price was 55 cents.[4]

Leisure and sport were also part of this initiative—unsurprisingly, as FDR was a sports fan who believed that games benefited Americans "physically, mentally and morally."[5] Furthermore, before he contracted polio in 1921, Roosevelt was an enthusiastic golfer, especially during his days at Harvard and when he was assistant secretary of the navy. By all accounts he was a long, if somewhat erratic hitter. However, his illness did not end FDR's enthusiasm for the game. Having contracted polio, he went to the Warm Springs spa in Georgia (a property he eventually bought) and, during his period of recovery, oversaw the construction of the nine-hole Warm Springs Memorial golf course. While the celebrated Donald Ross designed the course, FDR was regularly consulted. Roosevelt's strong connections with the game were also in evidence during his presidencies, notably when donating a brassie (no. 2 wood) of his to the Burning Tree Club, Bethesda. The club immediately found a place of honor in Bethesda's trophy cabinet.[6] In the 1930s, Roosevelt's enthusiasm for the game, and its democratization, was recognized when a WPA-funded municipal course in Philadelphia was named in his honor. The FDR course in Philadelphia is still thriving.

So sports in general, and golf in particular, were not surprising aspects of WPA policy. An ambitious program was devised which would provide work for thousands of laborers and which would make available much-needed facilities. One report stated that a total of 140,000 jobs were created in the leisure program: 100,000 men from the Civilian Conservation Corps worked on state and national parks and another 40,000 built facilities including athletic tracks, armories, and tennis courts.[7] Numerous swimming pools were also built as part of the WPA program, as was a zoo in Woodland Park, Seattle. Women's softball also flourished as hundreds of new parks were built, with many containing floodlit facilities which were ideal for night-time games. The WPA also inadvertently contributed to the nation's interest in body building. This happened on the beaches of Santa Monica, where the WPA set up a stage, gymnastic bars, and rings. The resultant interest in the "body beautiful" led to the local Santa Monica beach being called "Muscle Beach." The WPA also started a circus, which at one time gave employment to an out-of-work acrobat called Burt Lancaster.

While the twin aims of providing work and benefiting Americans "physically, mentally and morally" may have been achieved, there is little doubt that the WPA initiative had a third effect: that of engaging more Americans with sport. It is one of the paradoxes of the Depression years that while on the one hand professional sports were especially affected by a lack of money for salaries and prize money, on the other hand the public was starving for an outlet from everyday life. These new sports facilities at little cost to the participants provided just this release. Golf, too, would benefit from the WPA program, as the construction of hundreds of municipal golf courses—"the munys"—offered many an affordable escape from the realities of the Depression and helped popularize the game. As George B. Kirsch records, the government initiative saw "an increase in popular participation on public courses and the expansion of public golf facilities for the enjoyment of present and future generations. Thus the great cloud of the country's economic crisis contained a silver lining for the lovers of the Scottish game."[8]

It should be noted that the construction of public courses in America did not begin during the Great Depression. The year 1895, in fact, saw a nine-hole public course opened in Van Cortlandt Park, New York. *The New York Times* correspondent suggested that the course "will give satisfaction to all who want to try their skill over it."[9] The following year, Scottish architect Tom Bendelow designed a further nine holes in a project which also included extensive locker room facilities. More public courses would follow in the early decades of the following century, with considerable support in this regard coming directly from the White House.

Golf has had a long association with the American presidency, with presidents Eisenhower, Kennedy, George H.W. Bush and Clinton among the most active practitioners. However it is widely believed that William Howard Taft was the first golfing president. Weighing 300 pounds, Taft did not necessarily look like a golfer but there was no doubting his enthusiasm. According to Grantland Rice, he shot somewhere between 97 and 100.[10] Despite opposition from political advisors and some voters (who thought the game immoral, especially if played on Sunday), Taft undertook the role of popularizing the game and in 1913, he made a strong case for the creation of more public courses. "I hope to see the time," he wrote, "in the not far distant [future] when public golf courses will be offered to the public as in Scotland for costly golf privileges. I would have the funds raised by taxation. Golf is pre-eminently a game for the people and they should be allowed to play it. Properly played it brings a self-restraint that not even the churches can exert."[11] Suggestions that such courses should be paid for by taxes is not what might have been expected from a Republican president and it is hard to estimate exactly how much influence Taft had. However, the fact is that this decade and the next saw an increase in the number of public courses; figures show that by 1930, there were 543 "Munys" in America.[12] Notwithstanding this, it is fair to suggest that it was in the 1930s that public courses (and the game) achieved a much broader class appeal.

A prominent example of the New Deal municipal golf course plan was the Mark Twain Golf Course at Elmira, New York, designed by Donald Ross. Ross hailed from Dornoch, Scotland, where he learned the art of club-making and green-keeping, and it was here he first took an interest in course design. One of many golfing Scots to travel to the New World around the turn of the century, he became the most prolific course designer in America. At its peak, Ross's company employed 3,000 people. His resume included Oakland Hills, Seminole, and Pinehurst No. 2. He also served as head professional at Pinehurst. The Mark Twain course, which was located near the author's home, was officially opened in May 1937 with an exhibition of fourball which included Walter Hagen. The attendance was 2,000. Like numerous other WPA projects, Elmira did not just house a golf course, as the project also comprised a pavilion with men's and women's changing and shower rooms and a proshop, complete with living quarters above. A resident of Elmira could get a year's golf at the club for $15 while a nonresident was charged $20 per annum.

Ross also designed a municipal course at Asheboro, North Carolina. Here much of the work on the nine-hole course was done with hand-operated and horse-powered scoop pans. Ross projects were also completed at Triggs, Rhode Island, as well as the George Wright course in the working-class district of Hyde Park, Boston. For a man with his credentials, this may have seemed a step down. However, perhaps seeing the commercial possibilities in these harsh times, Ross was quick to champion municipal courses. "There is no good reason why the label 'a rich man's game' should be hung on golf," he said. "The development of municipal courses is the outstanding feature of the game in America today. It is the greatest step ever taken to make it the game of the people, as it should be.... I am naturally conservative, yet I am certain that in a few years we will see golf played much more generally than it is even played now."[13]

Ross was not the only course designer of note to take part in the WPA program, as the talents of A.W. Tillinghast were also used. Tillinghast, however, took a different view of the WPA program. Tillinghast, whose portfolio included Baltusrol and Winged Foot, was one of the era's more colorful figures and someone who very much fit in with the "roaring twenties." During this decade, he combined his design work with the role of a Broadway impresario and socialite. He was also a heavy drinker. Like many, however, Tillinghast lost out after the Wall Street crash, although his failed efforts as an impresario also con-

"Tillie," A.W. Tillinghast, noted course designer and editor of *Golf Illustrated* (courtesy Baltusrol Golf Club).

tributed to his financial difficulties. And like Donald Ross, he was happy to take on work from the government-funded public course initiatives. In this regard, one of his creations was the Bethpage Black course on Long Island, which has been in the news in recent years because of the USGA's decision to hold the National Open there. It has also attracted publicity because of a suggestion that the course designer was in fact course superintendent Joe Burbeck, with Tillinghast acting as a consultant. According to Charles McGrath of *The New York Times,* "For Tillinghast fans who tend to be passionate in their devotion, this is a little like arguing that Shakespeare didn't write *The Tempest.*"[14] Notwithstanding the disagreement, Bethpage is generally regarded as Tillinghast's work, certainly by the USGA and the Bethpage officials. Overall, the WPA initiative at Bethpage saw five courses built. In addition, the Bethpage project included a "colonial clubhouse, 358-feet-long ... locker rooms, men's and women's lounges, grill room. The furniture, copied from the American periods, was constructed entirely by relief labour."[15]

The reference to the women's lounge is significant, as many of the aforementioned new converts to the game during the 1930s were women, and many of the WPA projects had appropriate facilities. In addition, equipment manufacturers were paying more attention to the women's market; Helen Hick's clubs by Wilson (made to suit a woman's height) were very popular in this regard. Babe Zaharias turned professional in 1936 and promoted a range of clubs and balls made by Goldsmith. For the more fashion-minded player, the Walter Hagen Golf Company offered women's clubs with gray suede grips and gray Bedford cord golf bags to match. As with the men's game, $7 for woods and $5 for irons appear to have been popular prices. Interestingly, for women golfers, a set of 1936 Hagen clubs comprised two woods, six irons and a putter, at a time when the legal limit of 14 clubs maximum was still two years away.

For his Bethpage masterpiece, Tillinghast was paid $50 a day for a maximum of 15 days—much lower than his fees of earlier days, but times were hard. In a sad irony, however, it appears that Tillinghast did not share the ideals of the New Dealers. A staunch Republican, in 1942 and shortly before his death, he condemned these relief projects as the "generally ridiculous efforts of the WPA.... Doubtless the idea had some merit but much real harm was the result. For, Good Lord, when I review it all I can only regret the waste of so much good money and the resultant amateur accomplishments."[16] Thankfully, history proved him wrong: Bethpage was neither a waste of money nor amateur, and neither were the WPA-funded Perry Maxwell designs at Prairie Dunes and Southern Hills. These courses would go on to host the Curtis Cup and the National Open, respectively, and both were funded by the New Deal's WPA program.

Other ventures included the Little Rock Kiwanis Club in Arkansas. The construction of this course began in 1928 and while some holes were added in the coming years, it was not until the WPA and relief workers took over toward the end of 1937 that the work was fully completed. This comprised an 18-hole course; a two-story, stone clubhouse with facilities for men and women; and sprinkler systems. A small greens fee was required for all except members of the golf teams of local colleges and schools. It was reported that the income paid the upkeep of the course and provided a revenue for the city.[17] The WPA also ventured into college golf, as with the opening of the Iowa State course in May 1938. Here, Athletics Director George Veenker engaged the services of noted course designer Perry Maxwell. Veenker stated that "without the assistance and cooperation of the WPA, Iowa State College would today not have this fine recreational area."[18] Today, the course is named after George Veenker.

Texas also benefited from the WPA program with the opening of Houston's Memorial Park in 1936. This course was the creation of John

Bredemus, who was a significant figure in the history of Texas golf. Originally from the East, Bredemus was a man of many parts. An athlete and football player of note at Princeton, he competed in national golf tournaments both as an amateur and as a professional. While he did not become a successful player, over time he acquired a reputation as a teacher. He was also co-founder of the Texas Open and the state's Professional Golfers' Association. However, course architecture formed the greatest part of his golfing legacy, with Ben Hogan's Colonial, which he co-designed with Perry Maxwell, being his most significant achievement.

The Memorial Park project saw 500 men employed and a total cost of $184,166, of which only $29,601 came out of Houston city funds. Work began in 1935 and the first holes were built with one tractor and 20 teams of mules. The course officially opened in June 1936, with greens fees of 35 cents on weekdays and 50 cents on weekends. In general, the cost of golf at WPA courses ranged from 25 cents for 9 holes to 35–50 cents for 18 holes. Determining exact levels of disposable income during this time is difficult, but when we consider, for example, that the monthly rates of pay for WPA workers ranged from $40 for unskilled to $75 for skilled, it would appear that a weekly round of golf was an affordable past-time for many. The scale of the WPA golf initiative can best be gauged by the fact that in 1936 alone, 247 projects were ongoing, comprising new 9- and 18-hole ventures and the updating of existing courses. The government's golf outlay was $5.5 million during this year.[19] The program was also geographically comprehensive, with projects in approximately 40 states ranging from Wyoming to Florida and from the Bronx to California. In total, from the WPA's inception in 1935 to the end of 1939, *Golfdom* recorded that "500 modern, sporty public courses with a total of more than 6,000 holes have been made available to golfers in nearly every state by the Federal work relief programme."[20]

The WPA project received the approval of Bobby Jones, who was co-opted by Harry Hopkins as an advisor. It is important to point out that Jones had a commercial interest in popularizing the game, as he was the signature player of A.G. Spalding & Bros., market leaders in the field of golf equipment. Indeed, this was not the first time that Spalding had shown its nous in regard to seeing the link between an increased number of courses and its own commercial growth. At the turn of the century, for example, the company signed up course architect Tom Bendelow to promote the Spalding name, as his design career blossomed in both the public and private spheres. Up to his death in 1936, it was estimated that Bendelow designed 500 courses in the United States and Canada. Among these was Medinah, where the National Open, PGA Championship and Ryder Cup have been played.

For his part, Jones observed that this WPA initiative "will go a long way toward reducing the cost of the game for the average person. That is what is needed to popularize the game."[21] As noted, popularizing the game suited both Jones and Spalding. The more people who played the game, the more clubs and balls would be in demand. In May 1936, Spalding sent Horton Smith, Jimmy Thomson and Lawson Little on an exhibition tour aimed at the "democratization of golf." (Harry Cooper would later join the team.) Typically, an exhibition day would begin with a clinic in which the stars would demonstrate a range of shots; they would then proceed to play an 18-hole match. Admission was free of charge. Jones did not play, but he backed this effort, which took place almost exclusively at public courses, claiming "the potential development of public course jobs for pros qualified to expertly operate a public utility, legitimate promise of millions of dollars increase in pro income during the next decade."[22] While there is little doubt that this initiative was a smart piece of marketing aimed at increasing Spalding's business, the use of the word "democratization" fit in neatly with the mood of the time. All told, for the three years of this venture (1936–1938), the foursome traveled 100,000 miles and visited every state in the Union, as well as Canada and Mexico. Furthermore, the tour attracted over 300,000 spectators in total, all of whom attended the exhibitions free of charge.[23]

Whatever the commercial benefits both to himself and to Spalding, Jones was right: as noted, the game did become more affordable and, as a result of these popularly- priced greens fees, many new converts were attracted to the game. Just as important, however, were local government initiatives designed to kindle interest in golf. For example, Cincinnati's Public Recreation Commission, in tandem with the *Cincinnati Daily Post,* sponsored golf lessons in schools, local community centers, department stores and industrial plants. These lessons included a lecture on the history, etiquette and rules of the game. According to *Golfdom* magazine, they were instrumental in seeing 11,500 players registered on the two municipal courses in 1936, compared to 4,000 in 1934.[24] In many ways these combined efforts by local and national government led to the start, at least, of the true democratization of golf.

One further indicator of how golf was increasingly becoming a game for all the people could be seen in the staff policy of the giant International Business Machines Corporation (IBM). In 1935, IBM president Thomas J. Watson purchased a nine-hole course for his employees near

Pinehurst liked to advertise itself as the place where "there ain't no Depression" (courtesy Tufts Archives, Pinehurst, North Carolina).

the company headquarters at Endicott, New York. According to *Golfdom* magazine, almost the entire workforce of 4,000 used the course regularly, with the result that a new 18-hole course was designed by the prolific golf architect John Van Kleek in time for the 1937 season. Excellent facilities for both men and women were built and staff employees and their families were entitled to free lessons. It was recorded that over 2,000 lessons were given in the first year of this program.[25]

For what could be termed the traditional American golf world, a mixed picture emerged. Pinehurst in North Carolina, for example, which liked to advertise itself as "the place where there ain't no Depression," fared relatively well during the 1930s. Founded by the Tuft family just

Donald Ross, the famed course designer photographed at Pinehurst, where the No. 2 course is regarded as perhaps his greatest achievement (courtesy Tufts Archives, Pinehurst, North Carolina).

before the turn of the century, Pinehurst quickly became America's leading winter leisure center and its attractions certainly fit the mood and spending power of the 1920s. Apart from golf, amenities included cottages, a department store, a race track, dog kennels, polo fields, hunting preserves, and a gun club. Indeed, Annie Oakley competed in shooting contests there during the 1920s. Sport was seen as a way to attract people and the resort in general benefited from this. However, when the Depression came, a number of these pursuits were either discarded or reduced to save costs. In addition, at the resort's Carolina Hotel, staff wages were cut and the daily food plan was reduced from $2.73 to $2.[26]

Golf, however, was seen as profitable and as the resort's best chance of riding out the Depression years. To be sure, some cost-saving measures were introduced, such as resident professional Donald Ross accepting a $1,000 reduction in his annual salary. As well as being universally known as America's leading course designer—he designed four courses at Pinehurst—it is easy to forget that Ross was also a professional golfer of some standing and was good enough to win three North and South tournaments in addition to finishing fifth in the 1903 National Open. But in regard to costs, Pinehurst was fortunate in that it had its very own relief system, which was largely funded by donations from wealthy patrons. One program saw caddies (both black and white) receive a dollar a day for toting bags *and* working on course maintenance.[27] Partly as a result of this *and* prioritizing golf as a tourist attraction, the 1930s saw the greens at Pinehurst improved, with the introduction of rye grass greens which were eminently suitable for winter golf.

However, if Pinehurst survived (and it was about survival) better than most, overall there is little doubt that the Depression had a major impact on golf club revenues, with membership numbers estimated to have fallen by up to 65 percent.[28] One of the burdened clubs was the Salem Country Club in Massachusetts, which was deeply affected by the Depression. During the later stages of the 1920s, it was recorded that "the atmosphere of the locker room and the 19th Hole was robust and rollicking. The golf course, the dining room, the card room and the parking lots were bulging with membership—the membership was at its peak. In September, 1928, the membership reached a figure of 526 members." However, it was also noted that by the winter of 1930–1931, "the membership began to crumble and slip away."[29]

"The resignations came in slowly at first, but before the season was opened, the secretary was buried with an avalanche of letters so that by the end of the year, the loss of members became the major concern of the entire Board of Governors."[30] In 1933, for example, 111 members resigned their membership. Interestingly, the club had earlier taken the initiative by refusing to allow members to resign. Rather, they could go on the "Inactive List," whereby a payment of $5 allowed them to remain a member without playing rights until matters improved. But despite this and sacrificing entrance dues, numbers continued to slide.[31]

And it seems that all regions of the country were affected. Over on the West Coast, for example, the Inglewood golf club in Seattle also suffered. In 1926, to become a full member, a stock of $300 plus an initiation fee of a further $300 was required. By 1930, however, the initiation fee fell from $250 to $150 and by 1932, this would stand at $10. However, it was in the area of club personnel that the impact of the Depression was felt most keenly. This was before FDR's New Deal and in the days when there was little legislation in the workplace. In 1931, and in one sweep, most of the predominantly male staff were replaced by women, because they were less expensive. For example, the club chef, whose salary was $200 per month, lost his job to a woman who was paid $125. The following year, that position paid $100 per month. By 1937, however, with the Depression lifting, the monthly salary had moved up to $130.

The club professional at Inglewood was also affected. This was the English-born Walter Pursey, who was a player of some standing. Indeed, he finished 13th in the 1921 British Open and enjoyed a great deal of local success in the Pacific Northwest district when he came to Inglewood. In 1932, however, he had his salary reduced from a monthly figure of $188 to $100, although he did have the benefit of a club house. Furthermore, his honorary membership was canceled but he was allowed to continue selling golf balls. As was in line with the improving times, his salary moved up to $150 per month by 1937.[32]

Even some of the nation's most illustrious clubs suffered. Nowhere was this more in evidence than in the Chicago District, home to Medinah, Flossmoor, Olympia Fields, Glen Oak, and others. Charles Bartlett, golf editor of the *Chicago Tribune,* wrote of the impending trouble for golf clubs under the heading: "Economy to Rule in Golf Soon."[33] Bartlett went on to say that "Budget books and adding machines have been joined with drivers and putters in preparation for the opening of the 1932 golf season."[34] Bartlett did not exaggerate. Medinah, for instance, regularly hosted prestigious tournaments during the Depression years, such as the Western Open, and in later years it would hold both the PGA and U.S. Open championships. However, the early 1930s saw a continual fall in membership numbers, despite a reduction in both affiliation and initiation fees. For instance, between 1934 and 1939, numbers dropped from 1,100 to 592. Some novel solutions were required and like certain other clubs, Medinah turned to gambling to raise funds—slot machines, to be precise. These were located in the bar and men's locker room and records suggest that if it had not been for these machines, the club would have lost $200 in 1935.[35] The one-armed bandit may have seemed an unusual step, as the club was founded by Shriners (a form of free masonry) from the nearby Medinah Temple and the club had a strong moral dimension. Indeed in the year the slot machines appeared, the local Methodist minister held Sunday School meetings in the Medinah clubhouse for the children of parents who played golf on the Sabbath rather than listen to the good book.[36] In 1935, all proceeds from the $3,000 Medinah Open won by Harry Cooper went to the Shriners' Hospital for Crippled Children. However, with the club's financial standing in such doubt, gambling was deemed a legitimate indulgence.

Flossmoor was another of the district's more prestigious clubs and was home to both the PGA championship and the National Amateur during the 1920s. However, it, too, was forced to make a number of adjustments during the early 1930s to combat falling revenue. For example, to attract guests, green fees were reduced from $3 to $1 per day. The club also arranged for reduced bus fares from the nearby railway station to the course. Similarly, Glen Oak Country Club had a membership roll of 300 in 1929 and a waiting list of 35. However, by 1932, the membership stood at 145 and there was no waiting list. It took Glen Oak until the end of the decade before its membership numbers returned to 1929 levels.[37]

Nor was Olympia Fields immune from these harsh times. Despite being the site of the 1925 PGA Championship and the 1928 National Open, this famous club had to come up with its own innovative ideas to combat the times. One of these was a policy whereby existing members "could rent their membership to a suitable non-member."[38] The club also reduced the cost of meals and cut the Sunday greens fee from $5 to $3. There were, however, signs of a revival by 1934, with the club reporting 150 new members and greens fees up fourfold compared to the same month in 1933.[39]

In the east, famed Baltusrol, the scene of many major championships, was not immune from the times. The 1930s saw the club lose a third of its membership, with numbers falling from 650 before the Depression to 450 by 1934. As a result, initiation dues were waived for a period. Overall, the club saw its revenues decrease by 44 percent.[40] As with many other clubs, reducing operating costs was seen as a way of combating the Depression. In this regard, Baltusrol was fortunate in having Major R. Avery Jones as club manager at this time. Originally the club's greenkeeper, Jones not only worked for a reduced salary but also "showed a keen instinct for sniffing out bargains."[41] One such example was his purchase of 1,000 evergreen trees which he got for 10 cents each. Furthermore, he managed to persuade FDR and Harry Hopkins's WPA to plant them. The trees went on to become a feature of Baltusrol, adding definition to many of its holes.

Overall, despite some optimism as the decade reached its midway point, there is little doubt that the early Depression years especially negatively impacted golf clubs and their incomes. The trend in membership figures was hardly surprising, considering the drop in disposable income experienced by many Americans. This was in sharp contrast to the prosperous 1920s, when golf boomed and when it was not unusual for keen golfers to belong to more than one club. A further practical example of these changed times could be seen at the A.W. Tillinghast–designed Suburban Golf Club in New Jersey, which saw a significant drop in membership and which, in 1934, reduced its annual dues from $150 to $100 per annum. Furthermore, to save costs, members took to weeding, greens cutting and general course maintenance; club employees took a cut in wages; and caddies were obliged to contribute 10 cents per bag from their fees to the club coffers.

Arguably, the caddie issue was a very accurate barometer regarding the financial health of golf clubs during this period. Long before golf carts and trolleys, caddying was an integral part of the game and an invaluable source of income for many families. Unlike in Britain, where caddies were often experienced practitioners, in America caddying was usually the preserve of teenage boys or men in their very early twenties. In these uncertain times, caddies might be the main breadwinner for the family while the father was unemployed.

The issue certainly came to the fore in the early 1930s, when many caddies felt they were not just being asked to take a drop in wages from perhaps $1 to 75 cents per round, but also being undercut by older men who had lost their jobs because of the Depression and were happy to take a job bag toting. For example, *The Chicago Daily Tribune* recorded, "It has been noted that adult caddies are more numerous on more courses to the south than to the north and west. This is attributed to the fact that steel towns to the south are on the beat of a great many floating labourers who turn to caddying when unable to find work in the mills."[42] Furthermore, club members were themselves cutting costs. One caddie even turned to print to put the caddie's predicament into perspective in a poignant letter to his local newspaper: "Now that the fall is here and the weather is getting cooler, fewer players are coming out and those who do dispense with the caddie. At Medinah where I caddie, on last Wednesday between fifteen and twenty four foursomes carried their own bags."[43] The writer went on to tell the readers that most of the caddies came from Chicago and explained how the trip out to Medinah involved a 30-mile journey in the hope of making a dollar. He suggested a "caddie unemployment day" to compensate for the loss of income caused by members carrying their own bags and by the competition from the unemployed.

The issue of unemployed men was also in evidence at prestigious Oakmont, home of numerous championships, where it was reported in 1931 that many older men were turning to caddying to put bread on the table. One report suggested that out of 235 caddies registered at the club, 50 percent were older than age 20, with two grandfathers included in this group.[44]

A further example of these changed times was found in Westchester County, where the local unemployment bureau received roughly 100 applications for caddying jobs in the area. Among those applying were business men, tree surgeons and architects. There was a certain irony here, as some women golfers complained that their new caddies were not as good as their regulars and asked that they be properly trained.[45]

The more serious side of the situation, however, saw a number of caddie strikes break out in protest at the reduced pay and the "new arrivals." One of these took place at the Butler course in the Elizabeth Township, Pennsylvania. In May 1932, a caddie strike took place when the course owner J.W. Butler ordered that round charges be reduced from 90 to 75 cents. Upon this news, one of Butler's businesses premises was set on fire. The strike was eventually settled with the assistance of 10 deputy sheriffs, five state policemen and some local firemen. The caddies went back to work for 90 cents per round. Another club where the police were enlisted was the "swanky" Exmoor Club at Highland Park. Here, some of the striking caddies adopted a novel way both of protesting and gaining publicity for their cause. They went nude and splashed in water hazards as well as jeered at the members as they played.[46]

However, despite these stories of hardship, there is contrasting evidence that for some, at least, very little changed. For example, the golf publications of that time portray an America far removed from the harshness of the Great Depression, with numerous photos of handsome and tanned men and women posing at a golfing event in Florida or the equivalent latest "hotspot." *The Amateur Golfer* carried articles by Jones and

Sarazen alongside reports on bridge, hunting, polo, property and the latest debutantes. *Golf Illustrated* advertised the latest golfing fashions from Saks, not to mention carrying pages of advertisements for exotic holidays from Palm Beach to the Caribbean to Venice to Gleneagles. Domestic golfing breaks also featured heavily, as in one piece under the heading "Motoring Among Southern Links." Here the reader was advised, "When the frost is on the pumpkin and the golfer has to wear gloves and a windbreaker, he begins to think of sunny lands where he may play."[47] In this case the recommendation was that he played in historic Virginia. If you fancied something different again, you could read about "The Golfer and His Yacht."[48]

Golf Illustrated also showed many photographs of glamorous women in the latest golfing attire under the heading of "Seen at the Country Club." Indeed the same magazine took up the spirit of the age by suggesting that "golfers who were fed up with depression talk" could get a "new deal ... with a set of new quality clubs" ... which would "lift our spirits."[49] It is fair to suggest that the editors of these established journals were catering to the needs and the views of their readers.

Advertisements also appeared in the newspapers, with the Cunard Line being particularly prominent in this regard. One cruise to the West Indies and South America, for instance, offered golfers the services of three professionals on board who would give regular demonstrations and who would hold a series of golf talks. There would also be driving contests from the deck with "all the balls used going finally to Davy Jones' locker."[50] Another Cunard advertisement, for a cruise to the Caribbean, offered silver trophies to the amateurs who won competitions arranged in the various stops en route.[51]

Against this mixed background of dwindling numbers in country clubs and yet more people playing the game, largely due the WPA program, how would the professional tour fare in the 1930s? How would it fit into a country with very different priorities than in the "Roaring '20s?" Certainly there was money to be made from golf and some of the seasoned professionals prospered—Gene Sarazen, for example, who would win both the British and U.S. Opens in 1932. Sarazen saw much of his fortune wiped out by the Wall Street Crash of 1929, but he enhanced his income by exhibition tours, often with trick shot artist Joe Kirkwood, and because of his long-standing association with Wilson Sporting Goods. Sarazen's great friend and rival, Walter Hagen, although entering the twilight days of his stellar career, could still command substantial fees for public appearances and exhibition matches.

Tommy Armour also did well during the Depression years. Armour won the British Open at Carnoustie in 1931, but it is fair to say that for the rest of the decade, his main source of income would come from teaching, at fees ranging from $50 to $100 per hour, notably at Boca Raton in the winter and Medinah for the rest of the year. Armour also profited from designing and endorsing clubs for Power Matched and more markedly from his famed range with MacGregor.

Overall, however, no one fared better than Bobby Jones. After his Grand Slam year of 1930, Jones retired and devoted more time to his law practice and to realizing the commercial potential of his status as America's favorite athlete. Because Jones did not wish to play competitive professional golf, the USGA granted him *non-amateur* status, so he could avail of his marketability but still retain his nonprofessional status. This issue was potentially contentious in that Jones could be seen to enjoy the best of all worlds. But his immense standing in the game on both sides of the Atlantic allowed him this *non-amateur* status with no damage to his reputation. Indeed, the decision of the USGA was fully supported by the Royal and Ancient (R&A), whose secretary Henry Gullen declared that "It would be somewhat absurd to take away the amateur status of a golfer who made money by producing verses on the game.... The question need never be raised as to his right to remain a member of the club."[52] Jones was a member of the R&A. He earned money from more than "verses on the game" and benefited from lucrative contracts with clubmakers Spalding and notably with Warner Brothers through a series of short, instructional movies. The strength of his enduring popularity with the American public and the amount of money still available in certain areas of life can be gauged by the fact that Jones received $120,000 for a series of 12 movies and a share of the profits if the gross take was over $360,000, which it was. Herbert Warren Wind, a fervent admirer of Jones, summed up the situation by accurately suggesting that "Jones' haul was pretty hard on the pros whom he had beaten as an amateur and now again as a professional."[53]

However, while Jones's face remained the most recognizable in the game, he was not a professional and therefore could not sell the tour. Although Sarazen especially and Armour and Hagen continued to be marquee names, they were making fewer appearances on the circuit. Against this setting, the PGA circuit would need to lean on the presence of some other faces. However, the tour would also need a more structured approach, and two men in particular contributed significantly to this: Bob Harlow and Fred Corcoran.

CHAPTER 2

The Golfing Czars:
Bob Harlow and Fred Corcoran

> *"Besides professional golfers, only rodeo contestants are willing to travel some 8,000 miles, pay their own expenses, receive no guarantees of being a dollar richer when they return. Every year some 300 trouping golfers jaunt from town to town, from coast to coast, making three-day stands in a carefully planned route known as the grapefruit circuit"*[1]—*Time Magazine*

As we saw in the previous chapter, the overall picture for golf at the start of the 1930s was very mixed and ranged from exclusive golf clothing at Saks, to many country clubs struggling to survive, to thousands of new converts to the game, to caddie strikes by those who were hard pressed to put bread on the table. As for tournament golf, there is little doubt but that golf suffered in the immediate wake of Bobby Jones's retirement. The profile which the game enjoyed in the print media was diminished, as was attendance at tournaments. The USGA conceded that in Jones's Grand Slam year of 1930, combined gate receipts for the U.S. Open and U.S. Amateur championships totaled $50,000, while in 1931, the figure was $20,000.[2] His absence, however, did not dilute either the media's or the public's fascination with Bobby, as he continued to make headlines. Everything from his Warner Bros. movies to his appearances in charity matches to the birth of his daughter was deemed newsworthy.

Notwithstanding this hangover, golf had to go on. In the case of professional golf and in an effort to make the organization more efficient and to raise the status of all of its members, the PGA underwent a number of changes during the early 1930s. Among these was the adoption of a code of ethics in 1932. Prominent in this regard was a request that players should enter events early, in order to give local sponsors sufficient time to use their names for promotional purposes. Golfers were also asked not to criticize tournament venues or to indulge in profanities. These measures were introduced to remind players of their responsibilities.

However, before the introduction of the code of ethics, the PGA appointed former Western Golf Association President Albert Gates as full-time business administrator in 1930. Gates was a respected figure and his appointment was broadly welcomed by the press. "Baseball has its commissioner, the movie industry has its general director and now comes the golf dictator"[3] was how one newspaper welcomed Gates. His selection was also seen as one that would be "far from planning any revolt from the constituted authorities of golf, such as the United States Golf Association," and he "would work with these bodies in keeping the game clean and sportsmanlike."[4] Understandably, Gates's major responsibility during these difficult times turned out to be looking after the interests of the club professionals, who accounted for the majority of the association's 2,202 members. Indeed, one initiative taken was to set up a relief fund for destitute professionals and their families. Working alongside Gates was Bob Harlow, who was purely in the business of trying to organize and promote tournaments, and there were ongoing tensions regarding priorities such as which group mattered most, the bread-and-butter professionals or the top players. These frictions would regularly surface during the coming years.

Bob Harlow was the son of a Congregational minister and came from a middle-class family in the prosperous coastal town of Newburyport, Massachusetts. He was a graduate of the University of Pennsylvania who bacame a journalist, where his work included general sports coverage. In 1921, he entered the world of golf when he became manager of Joe Kirkwood and more notably Walter Hagen. Much of his work at this stage involved setting up exhibitions for the flamboyant pair. He would later manage other professionals, including Horton Smith and Paul Runyan. Harlow not just had an eye for those like Hagen, who could "sell" golf, but could also recognize up-and-coming ability. As early as 1932, he forecast that a group including Laffoon, Metz, Guldahl and Hogan would win the national title within five years.[5] He had to wait a little longer where Hogan was concerned, but Guldahl won the title in 1937 and repeated the feat a year later.

By the start of 1930, Harlow and Walter Hagen had severed their official partnership, although Harlow did continue to arrange exhibitions for Hagen on an *ad hoc* basis. As Stephen R. Lowe records, "Hagen was looking to downscale his competitive activities; also, the PGA desperately needed a full-time event coordinator, and Harlow was a natural to fill the position." Lowe goes on to suggest that "the Hagen–Harlow separation, along with other events, signalled the devolution of Hagen's competitive career."[6] The comments about Hagen are instructive as they represent further evidence that whoever took on the job of selling the tour to the public, the sponsors, and the media would have to do so without guaranteed help from the man who, up to very recently, had been golf's greatest draw—certainly from the professional ranks.

Between 1930 and 1932, Harlow worked to develop the tour before he and the PGA briefly parted company, only to return in 1933. What was also significant was that in November 1933, it was announced that Gates would leave his post and return to his law practice. This was important because it allowed Harlow greater autonomy. However, the constant tensions which existed between the needs of club pros and the needs of those who were more interested in playing for a living were never far below the surface. These strains often became personal between Harlow on the one hand and PGA President George Jacobus on the other hand.

Jacobus was a highly influential and authoritative figure during this decade and possessed the added credentials of being a professional golfer himself, as opposed to being "just" an administrator. As head professional at the Ridgewood club in New Jersey, he had an excellent reputation as a teacher. In 1935, he also helped Byron Nelson's emerging career by taking him on as his assistant. Nelson's salary was $400 for the summer months and half of what he earned from giving lessons. Byron always credited his move to Ridgewood and the help he received from Jacobus as being very important stepping stones in his career. However, while Jacobus carried a great deal of weight in the professional game, the touring professionals to a large degree believed his first loyalty lay with the club pros; they still saw Harlow as the man best equipped to "sell" the tour.

In this regard, by cajoling local business leaders and chambers of commerce, Harlow managed to persuade enough sponsors as to the advantages of having the leading professionals turn up in their town, spend money in their hotels (often at a reduced rate for pros) and eat in their restaurants. On top of that, the town would gain a great deal of favorable publicity from having golf stars play on the local golf course. This in turn was bound to help the tourist business. The professionals, however, had to understand their responsibilities as well as the code of ethics noted earlier. Harlow was not slow to remind even the best of players that they were in the entertainment business and had to give value for money. "Golfers cannot do their best playing to empty fairways any better than actors can give a fine performance to empty chairs. You [the pros] are definitely in the show business and if you have any misgivings about the show business, buy a copy of the theatrical magazine, *Variety,* and absorb some of the atmosphere to be found in the pages of this journal of the masks and wiggers."[7] He also arranged radio and press interviews featuring the top players to further boost interest in tournaments and to help the always important attendance receipts.

Harlow's skills received indirect affirmation from O.B. Keeler, the good friend and Boswell of Bobby Jones. In late February 1932, Keeler traveled south to watch the Gasparilla Match-Play Open, which was sponsored by the Tampa Junior Chamber of Commerce and underwritten by 50 local business concerns, such as newspapers and hotels. Keeler deemed this a "worthy mode of achieving a good fast tournament in these parlous times."[8] The event was a success: the atmosphere at Gasparilla was deemed akin to that at Mardi Gras and Paul Runyan took home $925 for winning.

Harlow was also a visionary who saw the global importance of golf. When Walter Hagen's manager, he regularly traveled abroad with "The Haig" either to the British Open or on subsequent European exhibition tours. While these exhibitions were primarily money-making ventures for both manager and player, it would be wrong to see these trips purely in this light. Certainly when Harlow became tournament director, there is evidence that it was not just financial gain which motivated him in this regard. In November 1934, for example, he was instrumental in sending an American team to play a series of challenge matches against local Australian teams as well as to compete in some tournaments being held to celebrate Melbourne's centenary year. The team was made up of Paul Runyan, Craig Wood, Ky Laffoon, Denny Shute and Leo Diegel, and Harlow was quick to highlight the tour's "contribution to international sport." Harlow also wanted to "emphasize as strongly as possible that this is not a commercial undertaking. These men are giving three months of their time and the guarantee to date means no more than their expenses."[9] Certainly there was prize money to compete for, but the long journey without any guaranteed appearance money can be seen as a genuine attempt by Harlow to expand the game of golf. Subsequently, in 1935, he reversed the trend and brought a team of professionals from Japan to compete on the PGA circuit and to play in a series of exhibition matches. This progressive move brought effusive praise from journalist Francis J. Powers, who had briefly occupied the post of tournament director when

Harlow was removed in 1932. Powers wrote, "Should the United States ever be in need of an ambassador for international sweetness and sunshine, such as Great Britain has in Capt. Anthony Eden, your correspondent will recommend Robert E. Harlow now employed as high privy seal of the Professional Golfers' Association."[10]

And even in these difficult times, Harlow was promoting the idea of an all-year-round golf circuit. Some of this creativity was borne out of necessity, as a number of leading players had drawn Harlow's attention to the fact that good club jobs were not plentiful in the 1930s and that a summer/autumn swing to supplement the existing Grapefruit Circuit (November–April) might work. In truth, Harlow's dreams of an all-year-round tour took many years to come to fruition, although during this decade the circuit did expand, notably (as we shall see later) to the Pacific Northwest. In this regard, his foresight should be recognized and applauded.

It was also Harlow who initiated the practice of "blind draws" for tournament play. In 1932, Harlow argued that "it is unfair for a competitive golfer to seek special pairings or starting times and members of the PGA should not request committee chairmen for such ... each player should be willing to take the luck of the draw for partner and time."[11] Prior to this, golfers could make their own arrangements about time and playing companion and, in theory at least, gain an advantage regarding weather conditions and having an agreeable partner. In making his case, Harlow used the British Open as an example, arguing that golf's oldest championship was based on the premise that "all men are created free and equal" and where "every player is drawn from a hat and depends on the luck of the draw for partner and starting time."[12] While this custom did take a little while to filter through, in time it became accepted practice on the PGA tour.

Harlow was removed from his post in late 1936 after yet another falling-out with George Jacobus, the PGA president. This time it was alleged that Harlow was setting up a rival tour and that he had too many outside interests such as writing newspaper columns. Many of the leading professionals such as Runyan, Laffoon, Wood, Revolta, and Smith signed a petition demanding that he be kept on in the interests of the tour. The protest was to no avail, however, but on his departure, a fitting testimony to his contribution to professional golf was recorded in *The Lewiston Daily Sun.* "As late as 1922," the report went, "many capable golf pros were social outcasts at swanky country clubs in both the United States and England. They doffed their tweed caps to club duffers who couldn't break 100 but who had the dough. They brought their lunch to tournaments and to work and confined their social activities largely to raggedy caddies in their little shops. And then ... along came Harlow toting Walter Hagen with him. The lowly status of the golf pro changed to grandeur."[13] The word "grandeur" may have been an exaggeration, but there is no doubt that Harlow helped to greatly improve the image and well-being of professional golfers. He continued in golf, often writing newspaper articles, and he founded America's first weekly golf magazine, *Golf World*. For a time, he also helped promote Pinehurst as America's "top golf resort." His contribution to the game was officially recognized in 1988, when he was an inductee into the World Golf Hall of Fame, 34 years after his death.

Harlow's replacement as tournament manager was Fred Corcoran. In a number of ways, Corcoran was very different from his predecessor. Al Barkow described him as "Shanty Irish"[14] in a direct reference to his working-class, Catholic Boston roots. Barkow also acknowledged that in the best tradition of the Boston Irish, Corcoran knew how "to do politics."[15] Indeed, Corcoran was acquainted with the most famous political family from his home town, the Kennedys, and it was this capacity to "wheel and deal" that would serve him well for the rest of the decade and beyond.

Corcoran also had a wonderful grounding in golf, which began when he caddied at the local Belmont Club in Massachusetts. Indeed, at the age of 11, he was good enough to caddie for Alexa Stirling when the U.S. Women's Amateur Championshp was held at Belmont in 1916. Ms. Stirling, one of the first stars in women's golf, won the title. His golfing education was further enhanced in 1919 at the nearby Brae Burn Club, the site of that year's National Open. Corcoran went to Brae Burn expecting to caddie but was offered the job of bringing the players' scores back to the officials—something akin to a bookie's runner. Instead, because of his initiative, he ended up creating the first proper scoreboard for the U.S. Open Championship. This he did with the help of his brothers (he was from a large Irish family), who would run from the fairways back to Corcoran, who would then write the various scores on the board. There are two versions of which colors Corcoran used to show the player's scores. His daughter Judy claimed the colors were blue for pars, red for birdies, and green for bogies, while Al Barkow believed it was red for birdies, black for pars and brown for bogies.[16] Regardless, the important point was that for the first time spectators and journalists could easily identify where a player stood in relation to par. As for the scoreboard, it consisted of reams of butcher's paper tacked on to the wall of the clubhouse.[17] For this work, Fred was paid $5. This introduction into the big time eventually brought him into contact with some of the game's leading players, such as Sarazen and Hagen. He later honed his administrative skills as handicapper and secretary at the Massachusetts Golf Association (MGA). Furthermore, during his seven-year tenure with the MGA, he continued to operate the scoreboard for the USGA at both the U.S. Open and Amateur championships, a role through which he made invaluable contacts, notably among the press, which would serve him well in the years ahead.

So, while Corcoran differed from his predecessor in background, what he had in common with Harlow was an ability to sell professional golf as an arm of the entertainment business. However, his appointment was not universally welcomed by some of the established pros, many of whom had signed a petition to keep Harlow in his job. Horton Smith, for instance, who was a highly respected player and part-time tournament administrator, was particularly angry about Harlow's sacking and told Corcoran this. It should be noted that Smith was managed by Harlow, but he was not alone in his views. In contrast, the tour's "nice guy" Henry Picard (who admired Harlow's work) welcomed Crocoran.

In time, even the most hardened professionals saw Corcoran's qualities, even if some of his ideas were somewhat unusual. For example, he floated the idea of floodlight golf in an attempt to make it more accessible to the public. Corcoran argued that "In recent years about seventy per cent of the golf played in the East has been of the twilight variety. What's fantastic about the thoughts of thousands of office workers playing after dark, getting in 9 or 18 holes in the cool of the night. Night baseball once was thought a fantastic idea."[18] Despite the success of night baseball, the idea of golf at night never took off.

Corcoran also raised the question of doing away with the traditional "honor on the tee." Hagen and some other pros believed that the practice of whoever had "won" the previous hole playing first was outdated. However, this idea was strongly criticized by Bobby Jones and died a quiet death. On another occasion Corcoran arranged an exhibition fourball in which Jimmy Demaret, Gene Sarazen, Babe Ruth and Gene Tunney played with a six-piece band playing in the background. Corcoran's rationale was that golf was seen as being too formal and needed to appeal to a much broader audience. This idea did not catch on, but in later years he was asked by the U.S. Tennis Association for suggestions on how to make the game more popular. Corcoran had a ready-made answer: stop discriminating against professionals and make the game "open." At the time he was told that this would never happen, but history proved that he knew better than most what the public wanted. Similarly, in the mid–1950s, Corcoran campaigned to have golf included in the Olympics, claiming that as a truly international sport it belonged there. The idea did not gain much support but now, almost 60 years later, golf will be part of the 2016 games in Rio de Janeiro, further evidence of Corcoran's vision for sport and golf in particular.

As director of the tour, he was particularly adept at persuading local journalists to include stories about the forthcoming "stop" on the tour. He was also skilled in persuading sponsors to fund a local "Open," often by pointing out that 100 professionals would spend at least $100 per week, sometimes in a tournament with a $3,000 total prize fund.[19] The net benefit to the local economy was there for all to see. Corcoran, incidentally, was paid $5,000 per annum and $5 per day expenses, with his salary being underwritten by a $25,000 contribution the PGA received from the leading equipment manufacturers of the day.[20] Spalding, for example, was a leading donor to this fund.

Corcoran freely admitted he was fortunate in that within two years of his becoming tour manager, Sam Snead "exploded on to the sports pages."[21] Incidentally, in those days, Snead was referred to as a "dark haired youngster."[22] Corcoran quickly became Snead's manager and used the colorful "slammer" to enhance the tour's growing appeal. Indeed, one newspaper called Snead, "The fairway Moses who led the struggling pros out of the Depression to at least room and board."[23] This bout of hyperbole may have offended some of the day's established players, with whom Snead was not always popular. Regarded as something of a loner, Snead famously picked up after 11 holes of the 1938 Pasadena Open, by which stage he stood at seven over par. Even if he was not the first big-name player to do this, his fit of temper was frowned on by his fellow professionals. But he apologized and recovered, and there was no doubt that both fans and journalists saw Snead as a major attraction.

However, even without Snead, there seems little doubt that Fred Corcoran was destined to make a considerable impact on the PGA tour. By the end of the decade, prize money totaling $185,000 was on offer, compared with approximately $150,000 when he took over from Harlow. He went on to help start the LPGA tour and to co-found the Canada Cup—later the World Cup. He would also advise other top players such as Ken Venturi and Tony Lema. Like Harlow, Corcoran was inducted into the Hall of Fame. In his case he was honored in 1975, two years before his death.

By the end of the decade, it appeared as if Corcoran and Harlow had persuaded at least some of the city fathers that golf tournaments were indeed good for business. In Greensboro, for example, the sports editor of the local *Daily News* claimed that hosting the Greater Greensboro Open had "put our town on every sports page ... [it] ... was the greatest thing we've ever had ... [it was] ... open advertising for the city." Finally the writer (Laurence Leonard) went on to proclaim that "the gentlemen of the fairways are the fair-haired boys in our town."[24] Notwithstanding their huge efforts, however, the tour needed more than Harlow and Corcoran, and the next chapter will explore the development of the Grapefruit Circuit in some detail.

CHAPTER 3

The Tour 1931–1935

"Golf without Jones would be like France without Paris—leader-less, lightless, and lonely."[1]—Herbert Warren Wind on Bobby Jones's retirement in 1930

It was argued earlier in this book that one of the paradoxes of the Great Depression was that despite the economic hardship faced by many, participation in sports increased. This was largely due to the WPA-funded construction of thousands of sporting facilities, which made softball, gymnastics, swimming, golf, and a variety of sports affordable. At the macro level, interest in sports was also in evidence, and nowhere was this more apparent than in the Olympic Games of 1932 in Los Angeles. *Time Magazine* recorded that "observers who expected the Xth Olympics to be a failure because of Depression ... were vastly disappointed last week."[2] Record crowds came, with attendances of 105,000 in the L.A. Coliseum noted on certain days. In addition, America won 103 medals in total, almost three times as many as second-place Italy. Just as important as the collective success of the nation, however, was the emergence at the games of American sporting giants such as Babe Didrikson (later Zaharias) who took gold in the women's javelin and 80-meters hurdles. Indeed, it was a further irony that the 1930s saw sporting heroes in America assume even greater importance and status. It may have seemed rational to believe that with so many basic issues to contend with, such as food, a roof, and work, finding time to follow the sporting giants of the age would be far down the list of priorities. In fact, the opposite was the case and a list of all-time sporting legends captured the public's imagination. Included, apart from Didrikson, were Joe Louis, James J. Braddock, Lou Gehrig, and Joe DiMaggio.

41

Also included was Jesse Owens. Some comments from fellow athlete, and later national broadcaster, Marty Glickman, verify the point about the importance of sport during this era. Glickman was a sprinter who was selected for the 1936 Olympic Games in Berlin as part of the U.S. sprint relay team. In the event, Glickman was "removed" from the team due (it was alleged) to the fact he was Jewish; Owens replaced him and won one of his four gold medals as a member of the successful American team. Later in his career, when writing of the Depression era, Glickman said, "The sports heroes of the 1930s provided relief from the depression of the Depression. It was a tough time. There was a lot of unemployment and hunger, a lot of people on line for food. Listening to sports on the radio was one of the few enjoyments of the time." Sports historian John Lucas, writing specifically of Owens, suggested that "seeing another human being perform at an almost metaphysical level uplifted the human spirit. If only for the briefest time, people were inspired and forgot their problems."[3] As for professional golf and its fledgling tour, the remainder of this book will look at how people were inspired by the game's leading players and at what sustained the "Grapefruit Circuit" during the Depression years.

Golf journalists and historians have long enjoyed the symmetry of the trios that have at different times dominated the game—from the original Great Triumvirate of Vardon, Braid and Taylor, to the more recent Big Three of Nicklaus, Palmer and Player. In between these illustrious names, however, there were other threesomes which ruled the game in their eras. First were Jones, Hagen and Sarazen, who between them won 31 majors in the 1920s and 1930s. Some of the excellence of Sarazen and Hagen has already been noted and more will be covered in the pages that follow. Second was the more modern triumvirate of Snead, Nelson and Hogan. These players were all born in the same year (1912) and all emerged in the Depression era, albeit with different degrees of success. Nelson became a regular winner of tour events in the second half of the 1930s, as well has picking up two majors. Snead burst onto the scene in 1937 with a magnificent swing and homespun personality which was a gift for golf writers ever-eager for a quote. And if Hogan's great days belonged to the 1940s and especially the 1950s, he too learned the professional game during the 1930s. However, when taking an overall view of the Depression years, a strong argument can be made to the effect that there was no obvious star attraction such as Vardon, Jones, or Hagen had been in earlier years. This is not a widely held view and in this regard it is difficult to challenge the opinion of perhaps the most famous and most revered of all American golf writers, Herbert Warren Wind.

In his excellent biography of Hogan, Snead, and Nelson, *American Triumvirate,* James Dodson recounts a conversation he had with the author on Snead's impact on the game when he first came on tour. "Sam was an original," Wind said, " no question about it. That's what endeared him to so many at a time when the game desperately needed a bona fide star and headline maker. The tour was really struggling when Sam broke through out west and won a flurry of tournaments on the winter tour in 1937. He was a complete unknown, a plainspoken hillbilly from the Blue Ridge Mountains, as they portrayed him—but he gave golf a legitimate star at a moment when the tour could easily have gone under."[4] This is powerful language, especially the claim that but for Snead, the tour may have perished. Certainly there is little doubt of the drawing power of the colorful Snead ("the fairway Moses") but by the time he became a regular on tour, crowds were already healthy and Fred Corcoran had built on Bob Harlow's impressive legacy with the PGA. Certainly times remained tough, although the economy showed signs of better health, but the golfing facts, in terms of overall prize money and the number of tournaments, suggest that the Grapefruit Circuit was strong enough to survive. Furthermore, unlike Hagen and Sarazen, who were multiple major winners and the star attractions of the 1920s, Sam had yet to accomplish this feat. This did not happen until he won the 1942 PGA title.

As a matter of record, then, it is important to look at the many other professionals who either surfaced or became prominent during the Depression years. Some of these were and remain less well known than the aforementioned "greats" of the game; they were, nevertheless, wonderful players who enhanced and helped sustain the tour and who built up formidable records. We are talking here of names such as Denny Shute, Ralph Guldahl, Olin Dutra, Henry Picard, and Paul Runyan, all of whom were multiple major winners. Arguably, this group (and many others) helped sustain the tour during this era, and their stories deserve to be told just as much as those of their better-known peers.

A look at the logistics of the PGA circuit in the early Depression years shows that it was, as noted earlier, centered around those states with a pleasing winter/spring climate. For example, the 1931–1932 season began in early December in San Francisco, California, and ended in late March at Pinehurst, North Carolina. In between, stops were made at Texas, Arizona, Louisiana and most of all Florida. However, it was a venue outside America which captured the headlines at the start of the 1930s.

A glance at the PGA tour of the early 1930s might show a picture of events with purses between $2,500 and $5,000 (compared with some of $10,000 in the 1920s). Certainly in some instances this was the case. However, what was remarkable was that there were also purses which seemed out of step with the Depression era. Nowhere was this more in evidence than in Agua Caliente.

Agua Caliente was located across the Mexican border in Tijuana. In the early Depression years it was a playground for the rich and famous. With drinking, horse racing and gambling banned in nearby California, many Hollywood celebrities such as Charlie Chaplin, Buster Keaton and Bing Crosby made the relatively short trip to the gambling tables and the

The always "quotable" Leo Diegel (Photographic History Collection, Division of Information Technology and Communications, National Museum of American History, Smithsonian Institution).

race track, built at a cost of $2.5 million. One headline described how "Movie Stars Play After Work in Palaces of Agua Caliente." The reporter went on to note how he spied "Douglas Fairbanks eating a bite of lunch as he looks over the entries for the third race and ... Mack Sennett sitting at a roulette table playing 'ten' and 'twelve.'"[5]

The Hollywood connection was perhaps natural, as the movie mogul Joe Schenck was part-owner of the Agua Caliente complex. Schenck later became chairman of Twentieth Century–Fox. The legendary Australian horse Pharlap won a $50,000 prize for a handicap race at the track in 1932. Later, in 1938, the incomparable Seabiscuit, which lightened the gloom for many Americans during the Depression years, won the same race.

Professional golf also benefited from this largesse. To establish Agua Caliente as a golfing center, the club hired Leo Diegel in the late 1920s for the highly significant amount of $15,000 per year. This regular income was especially welcome for, as we know, along with Sarazen, Diegel lost out heavily during the Florida property crash of the 1920s.[6] Diegel was one of the era's most interesting personalities. In the early stages of his career he gave lessons to President Warren Harding, who did so much to popularize the game in the 1920s. Leo's duties in Agua Caliente included serving on the tournament committee. As befitted a man known for having strong opinions, he had some interesting suggestions on how to cope with slow play, which he believed was doing serious harm to the game. The notoriously slow Cyril Walker, Leo claimed, once took three and a half hours to play nine holes at the 1922 Southern Open in New Orleans, where Leo was also part of the organizing committee. At this time, the leaders did not go out last (as became the norm in later years) and Leo believed that deliberately sending the offenders to the back of the field was the answer. "I think that the twilight game for the slow pokes is the best cure. Those who are habitually slow are pretty well known by their brother players. The tournament committees could be acquainted with these facts and the habitual offenders could be given starting positions at the bottom. Then if they wanted to stay out all night they would be hurting only themselves. Make 'em finish too, even if they needed lanterns."[7] Leo practiced what he preached: he claimed that in that same Southern Open, after Walker's tardy nine holes, Diegel placed him at the back of the field the following day and Walker finished 90 minutes after the rest of the field had submitted their score cards. According to Diegel, this lesson helped Walker speed up and indirectly led to his winning the National Open title in 1924.[8]

Apart from holding forceful views, Diegel was also known for his "arms-akimbo" putting style, for his constant theorizing on the game, and for being the "nearly man" of the majors. The "nearly man" tag owed a great deal to the fact that on a number of occasions, Diegel came close to winning in both the U.S. and British Open Championships. The facts, however, were that he was a wonderful player with a significant tournament record, which included over 30 wins and most notably, two majors. In 1928 he was the man who stopped Hagen from winning five PGA titles in a row. From this base in Mexico, Diegel successfully defended his title in 1929 by beating Hagen in the semi-final and Johnny Farrell in the final.

Staging a big professional event was a natural progression for Diegel, and the Agua Caliente Open became the most lucrative stop on the winter tour. It was pure Hollywood, with local caddies dressed in traditional Mexican garb complete with gold braided jackets and "gaucho" hats. The money on offer was also "Hollywood." Played usually in January, the tournament offered purses of up to $25,000 with a hefty first prize. For example, in January 1931, John Golden defeated George Von Elm in an 18-hole play-off and won the first-place money of $10,000 plus a diamond-studded gold medal worth a further $1,000. Von Elm's second-place finish was officially $3,500, but it was widely believed that the two players divided the first- and second-place spoils, with each receiving $6,700. Golden may not

John Golden, who died relatively early in his career (courtesy USGA/George S. Pietzcker).

have been one of the "star" names from this era, but

he was a proven winner during the 1920s, when he was twice a Ryder Cup player and formed a successful foursomes pairing with Walter Hagen. Sadly, he died from pneumonia in 1936 at the relatively young age of 39.

Golden's win was also noteworthy for reasons other than the large first prize, as it highlighted the sometimes uneasy relationship between the leading amateurs and the professionals. There was no doubting the affection in which Jones was held by the public, nor was there any shortage of respect for him among the pros. However, his ability to regularly beat the professionals, even though he could not take home the first-prize money, was not overly welcomed by those in the paid ranks. And the media were quick to remind the professionals of Jones' superiority. For example, when "warming up" for his 1927 season, Jones finished eight shots clear of the pros in the Southern Open. One newspaper was moved to suggest that like brook trout in the angling world, "the professionals must be protected against Bobby Jones."[9]

And it was not just the loss of tournament prestige which bothered the professionals. During the late 1920s, when Jones was at his peak, some in the paid ranks claimed that "we can't get the fee for instruction that we could at one time because we are not as good as Jones."[10] In short, according to some pros, Bobby was making them look bad both on and off the course.

It was no surprise, then, that Golden's fellow professionals were very anxious that he beat George Von Elm in the play-off at Agua Caliente. Von Elm had a wonderful amateur career and only Jones ranked above him during the mid- to late 1920s. Indeed, he defeated Jones in the final of the U.S. Amateur in 1926. Von Elm was a recent addition to the professional ranks, having decided that he could no longer afford the $10,000 annual cost of playing the amateur circuit. He had strong views on the often blurred distinction between being an amateur and professional and he resented the fact that he could not make money from the vast crowds who watched, for example, the U.S. Amateur Championship. This resentment was exacerbated by the fact that Jones, as an amateur, was known to make significant money from his newspaper columns. Perhaps there was some jealousy here, as Jones had long been America's favorite athlete and no golfer could match his drawing power, on or off the course. In addition, Jones and Von Elm did not like each other.

So Von Elm became what the media described as a "businessman golfer." What this meant was that he had little interest in taking up the regular professional duties, as was the norm for even the best players; he was not prepared to pay his dues. Instead, Von Elm was purely interested in prize money. This approach did not sit well with the PGA members and *The Pittsburgh Press* described the reaction to Von Elm's windfall as follows: "Always clannish to a degree, the professionals were none too pleased over the unexpected appearance of Von Elm as a dominating factor in the shots-for-cash battalion."[11] The clannishness may have been understandable in these difficult times, but Von Elm proved himself to be a top-class professional player, as evidenced by his runner-up finish

The colorful ex-sailor, Wiffy Cox (courtesy USGA/George S. Pietzcker).

to Billy Burke in the National Open of that year—after a 72-hole play-off.

A further attraction for professionals crossing the border to Agua Caliente was a prize list which was more extensive than that offered in many other events, with 24th place receiving $50 in the early 1930s. In an era where tournament prize funds were often "front-loaded," this was not an insignificant sum. To be sure, this level of prize money was not maintained for the few years of the tournament's existence. But even in 1934, Wiffy Cox took home first prize of $1,500—a significant amount, considering that many tournaments offered the winner a three-figure sum.

Agua Caliente, however, was the exception and a look at some of the events in early 1931 makes for more mixed reading. For example, in early 1931, Joe Turnesa won the Miami Open from Johnny Farrell, with the undisclosed purse being made up of "entry fees, gate receipts and a $500 fund provided by the management."[12] The entry fees were usually $5. In January 1931, at age 19, a tall young Texan called Ralph Guldahl won his first tour event, when he beat Tony Manero in the final of the "Motion Pictures Open" in Los Angeles. For this he received $1,000.

Some events were better than others with, for example, Gene Sarazen typically finding form for the big-money events like the La Gorce Open at Miami Beach. Sarazen won the $5,000 first prize from the substantial total fund of $15,000. Craig Wood won the 36-hole stop at Harlingen, Texas, and the first prize of $1,000; for finishing as runner-up, Horton Smith took home $600. However, there was no safety net here. With the majority of the prize money going to the top six finishers, this meant that approximately half of the 47 golfers who teed up in Texas went home empty handed. Even when sharing cars and rooms, it was difficult for touring professionals to manage on less than $100 per week expenses, so making money was tough.

Like Agua Caliente, some tournaments distributed the prize fund more equitably. Fourballs were a regular part of the tour at this time and in the Miami event of spring 1931, Wiffy Cox and Willie MacFarlane received $750 each as winners, but the first-round losers got $50. Such events were rare, however, and front-loaded purses would remain a feature of many events during the decade. The winter circuit officially ended with the North and South Open at Pinehurst. As in Miami, the winner was Wiffy Cox, after a play-off with Joe Turnesa. Cox and Turnesa shared $1,500 from a total purse of $5,650, but overall there were only 15 prizes, the lowest of which was $36.66.

Wiffy Cox was one of many colorful players from this era. Chris-

tened Wilfred Hiram, Cox grew up in Brooklyn and was introduced to
the game as a caddie. Wiffy joined the Navy and saw service in World
War I, after which he returned to golf and became a professional. In the
early 1930s, he served as professional at the Dyker Beach (formerly Dyker
Meadow) public course in his native Brooklyn. As an ex-sailor, on occasions Wiffy was known to use "sailor's language" on the course, especially

Tom Creavy, the unheralded but deserving winner of the 1931 PGA title (courtesy
Wannamoisett Country Club).

when things did not go to plan. *Time Magazine*, always keen for an angle, also noted how at the following year's National Open, Cox "threw away his ball and then his putter" when easy putts were missed.[13] Byron Nelson, in contrast, saw another side of Cox, whom he found to be a very agreeable playing partner when playing with him in the final round of the 1937 Masters—Byron's maiden major victory.

Wiffy would go on to become a respected teacher in the game, notably at the prestigious Congressional club in Washington, D.C., where he became head professional in 1938. However, the following year he showed that some fires still burned within, when it was discovered that a number of skunks had eaten up parts of the Congressional course. Wiffy's answer to this outrage was to wait until dusk one evening and then shoot 33 of the offending animals. Unsurprisingly, animal welfare groups were not impressed.

By the end of April, the tour was winding down and some professionals returned to their club jobs, if they had one. However, while tour stops became less frequent, it did not mean the end of competitive golf for the year, as many important events were staged. The Masters did not begin until 1934, but the two original American majors took place, with Billy Burke winning the U.S. Open in July 1931 and the relatively unknown 20-year-old Tom Creavy winning the PGA title two months later. Apart from winning national titles, both victors were notable in other ways.

Tom Creavy, for example, was competing in a major for the first time and was only 20. His background was typical of the times, in that he and his brothers, who also became professionals, learned the game by caddying in Westchester, New York State. Tom started his professional life as assistant to his older brother Bill, who had become pro at the Bonnie Briar Club. Tom had certainly shown promise when, as a 17-year-old, he finished in eighth place in the Shawnee Open. However, when Creavy was drawn to play Gene Sarazen in the semi-final of the PGA, he was given little or no chance, even if, as was reported, his motivation to defeat his more illustrious opponent was particularly high. A few years earlier, Tom had watched Sarazen play an exhibition match at Oak Ridge, New York, where he often caddied. During the match, Sarazen turned to ask his caddie for advice on which club he should play. Tom, who was standing near Sarazen's caddie, piped up: "Try a mashie niblick shot." It was well known that Sarazen could be feisty, especially with those whom he felt had not earned their golfing spurs, so his response was no surprise: "What do you know about golf? Where did you learn the game?"[14] Tom, apparently, did not forget this put-down and easily won the match by 5/4. He then went on to beat Denny Shute 2/1 in the final and win the $1,000 prize. An additional feature of the Creavy–Shute match was that it was refereed by Bobby Jones. The practice of having a big-name player officiate at the PGA Championship was customary during this era. For example, Francis Ouimet was referee for one of the 1931 semi-finals and George Von Elm for the other. As it turned out, the PGA Championship was Creavy's only win of note, even if he did reach the semi-finals in his title defense the following year and figure prominently in other events. Creavy subsequently suffered from ill health but he enjoyed a very prominent teaching career in later life; he counted among his pupils Tommy Aaron, who would win the Masters in 1973.

Billy Burke's win made history in a different way, as he and George Von Elm were tied after 72 holes, and tied again after a 36-hole play-off, before Burke won by one in another 36-hole decider. Burke's story was a classic American tale and one that was similar to Gene Sarazen's story. Sarazen was born Saraceni into a poor Italian family and caddying was his entry into golf. Billy Burke was born Burkowski to Lithuanian parents who emigrated to America at the turn of the century. The family settled in Naugatuck, Connecticut, where Billy's father worked in an iron foundry. Billy discovered caddying at the age of 12 and, as a result of this, started playing golf. When he left school, he worked as a janitor and in a rubber company before following this father into the iron foundry. However, golf was his passion and after his shift in the iron foundry, he would resist the "sissy" jibes from his co-workers at the foundry and go and practice.[15] Billy tried his hand in local amateur events but when, as an 18-year-old, he wanted to compete in the most important one, the Connecticut Amateur, he was faced with a problem: he had no knickers (plus-fours). As *The Pittsburgh Press* was quick to point out, "What was a golfer without knickers?"[16] Fortunately for Burke, two local players for whom he caddied came to the rescue and provided him with the necessary attire and some new clubs and the fare to the tournament. Here, despite losing in the final, Burke enjoyed more good fortune, as his conqueror was Henry Topping. Topping was a leading amateur who had two wins in the prestigious North and South Championship in his golfing resume. He was also a millionaire businessman. Topping took an interest in the young Burke and helped him get started in the professional game. His protégé went on to win his country's greatest golfing prize as well as 12 tour events. He also played twice on the Ryder Cup team.

As for the 72-hole play-off, William D. Richardson covered the event for *The New York Times* and his report began on page 1, alongside reports of Stalin's New Economic Plan and of how President Hoover had to give up his Sunday dinner at his Rapidian retreat and rush back to Washington for debt talks. (The Rapidian Camp was built by Hoover and served as the presidential retreat in the pre–Camp David era.) Like Grantland Rice, Richardson covered a number of sports but arguably it was golf which defined his career. Also like Rice, Richardson was a much respected figure. Just after the war, it was in part his idea to found the Golf Writers' Association of America. After his death in 1946, an award bearing his name was initiated by the Association and presented annually to those deemed to have made a notable contribution to the game of golf. Among the recipients to date have been Jack Nicklaus, Tom Watson, Bing Crosby and Dan Jenkins.

Of the Burke–Von Elm battle, he wrote after the first 36 holes, "The long-waged wars of ancient times have nothing on the wars that linksmen are now waging in the National Open Championship."[17] Richardson later went on to give his readers a blow-by-blow account of how "the gladiators" handled the tough Inverness course. "First hole, Burke hugged the left

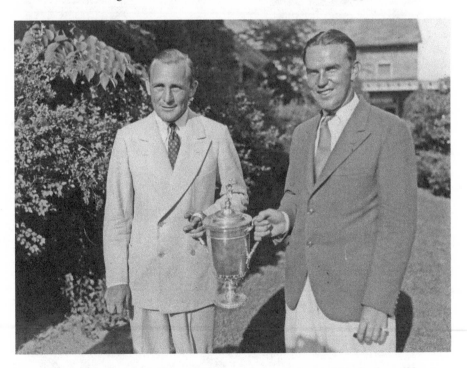

George Von Elm (on the left) and Billy Burke before their epic 72 hole play-off for the 1931 U.S. Open. (courtesy USGA).

side of the fairway with his drive.... Second hole, Von Elm drove into a bunker but played a gorgeous No. 2 iron onto the green ..."[18] From today's perspective, with the benefit of nonstop televised golf, this style may seem a little unnecessary. However, in 1931, such detail, complete with a card of the course, was essential in terms of giving the readers insight into the drama and challenges that came with trying to win America's greatest golfing prize.

The 1931 National Open was also notable for being the first time a

Walter Hagen, who continued to draw the crowds in the 1930s (courtesy USGA).

major championship was won by a player using steel shafts. The steel shaft had been legal in America since 1924 (1929 in Britain) but was not immediately adopted by the leading players, such as Jones and Hagen. However, at the start of the 1930s, players such as Horton Smith began to win with the steel shaft and it quickly became the choice of champions. Indeed, after his retirement, Jones regularly used the steel shaft when playing exhibition matches and went on to design steel-shafted clubs for Spalding.

During the summer of 1931 there were some other tournaments, such as the Canadian Open, in which Hagen achieved one of his increasingly rare wins. However, professional golf tournaments survived. As one of the game's oldest events (it started in 1904), the Canadian Open was a prestigious tournament which attracted top-class fields. The tournament also created great interest within the local media and among Canadian golf enthusiasts, who had few opportunities to see the game's top professionals in action. It was reported that between 8,000 and 10,000 spectators watched the 36-hole play-off in which Hagen defeated Percy Alliss, father of commentator Peter, whom *Time Magazine* called a "plump British professional."[19] A key to Hagen's victory, it was reported, was that after the morning round of the play-off, he discarded his usual

"Sir" Walter Hagen in regal pose (courtesy Tufts Archives, Pinehurst, North Carolina).

"Beau Brummel" attire and "played in loose fitting and comfortable toggery."[20]

The presence of Alliss at the Canadian, along with other British professionals, including Henry Cotton, came about indirectly because the Ryder Cup was held two weeks earlier at the Scioto Club in Ohio. In general, Ryder Cup years saw the visiting professionals play some tournaments in the host country. However, in this instance, Allis did not play in the Ryder Cup matches due to a dispute with the British PGA. Nor did Cotton or Audrey Boomer play, although each of the three merited selection. At this time, the British PGA insisted that all team members must not only be British citizens but must also reside in Britain. This ruled out Boomer and Alliss, who were attached to clubs in France and Germany, respectively. Cotton, however, became involved in a dispute with the British PGA by refusing to agree to share any fees gained from exhibition matches with the rest of the team and by his insistence on remaining in America after the matches. In a display of the independent

Fred Morrison, a fine player and brother of noted teacher Alex (courtesy the Palos Verdes Library, District Local History Collection, California).

streak which marked his career, Cotton instead asked Boomer and Alliss to join him on a tour of America and Canada. Clearly, despite the reference to his physique by *Time,* this proved to be a good move by Alliss.

As for the Ryder Cup, the U.S. team, captained as usual by Hagen, won the third holding of the matches by nine to three. In truth the British team was more or less defeated before the matches began, given the row over selection and further indications of low morale. For example, one member of the team, Herbert Jolly, withdrew before the team sailed for America, citing poor form as the reason. He was replaced by Arthur Lacey. Certainly the British press gave the team no chance, describing the players as a "bunch of has beens" and a "group of amiable middle-aged golfers."[21]

Apart from the occasional summer stop, such as that in Canada, it was really late October or early November before the tour started in earnest again, with almost weekly events. Among these was the Metropolitan match-play title at Long Island, which saw Paul Runyan beat Sarazen in the final and win $500. Each of the 16 first-round losers received $10.

These details provide a brief overview of how the tour operated during the early 1930s. Certainly, as we shall see later, there is evidence that the tour grew both geographically and financially from this point. However, the basic principles endured for a number of years: a predominantly winter/spring tour, a mixture of modest and very good purses, and prize funds which favored the high finishers only.

Early 1932 saw some clear evidence of the Depression biting, when it was announced that the Texas Open in January would carry a prize fund of only $2,500. By comparison, the purse was $6,000 when the inaugural event was staged 10 years earlier. Notwithstanding this, the annual golfing prize fund totaled roughly $100,000, with some large winners' checks on offer. As in the previous year, Agua Caliente made headlines with a huge $5,000 first prize on offer. This was won by the tall Californian Fred Morrison, who outplayed the formidable Sarazen in the closing stages. Apart from the prize money, Morrison's win was notable for being the first time that a local West Coast professional had outplayed the "big boys" from the East in a really important Californian event. Before this, according to Morrison's fellow Californian Olin Dutra, the local pros were fine when competing in their own local events, but once the star names came west chasing the big money, the West Coast players lacked the necessary belief to win. According to Dutra, "all of us were licked before we started." Olin directly credited Morrison's win with lifting his own inferiority complex when it came to competing against Sarazen,

Hagen and the rest. "If there was any doubt of this," he suggested, "Fred Morrison removed it when he won the Agua Caliente Open last January. I saw Fred win that title. I was playing with him and Sarazen the last day. I saw Fred cling to his lead and win."[22] According to Olin, this psychological breakthrough contributed to his becoming PGA champion later that year.

Apart from Tijuana, there were some other lucrative first prizes on offer. MacDonald Smith, for example, received $2,000 for winning in Los Angeles, his third victory there. At age 40, Mac Smith was coming to the end of what had been a wonderful career. As suggested earlier in this book, in the early decades of the professional game in America, to be considered a really worthwhile professional you needed to be Scottish. In this regard, Mac Smith was one of the many Scottish professionals to come to America in the late 19th and early 20th centuries, a group whose members had a profound impact on the development of the game in their adopted land. Jock Hutchison, for example, in 1921 became the first American-based player to win the British Open—fittingly on the Old Course, near the place of his birth.

The Foulis brothers from St. Andrews also made a significant impact in the early years of the professional game in America. James, for example, won the second National Open in 1896 and along with his brothers Robert and Dave, became prominent as a teacher and course designer in the Chicago region. (Dave's son, Jim, would win the St. Paul Open in 1933.) There was also Stuart Maiden from Carnoustie, who taught Bobby Jones, and Willie MacFarlane from Aberdeen, who defeated Jones in a play-off for the 1925 U.S. Open title. And there was Willie Anderson from North Berwick, who won four U.S. Open titles, a record that he shares with Jones, Hogan and Nicklaus and that remains unsurpassed.

The Smith family, from Carnoustie, was unique in that five brothers were professional golfers. Of these brothers, two—Willie and Alex—won three U.S. Open titles between them. The Smith's were also excellent teachers. Alex, for example, was a major influence on the career of Glenna Collet (later Glenna Collet Vare), who in the 1920s and 1930s was America's leading woman golfer, with six U.S. Amateurs to her name and a host of other titles.

Mac Smith was the baby of this golfing family and became one of the game's great stylists. However, despite this and a career which saw him achieve 24 tournament wins, he was often regarded as the "nearly man" of the majors. One of his near misses came at the 1910 U.S. Open when, as an 18-year-old, he lost a play-off to his brother Willie. John

McDermott was also in that play-off. More recently, he had come very close to stopping Bobby Jones from winning his Grand Slam, when he pushed him all the way in the National Open of 1930 at Interlachen. Smith eventually finished two shots back. In 1932, he would shoot the fine score of 288 at Prince's in the British Open, only to see Sarazen set a new championship record with 283. Again Mac Smith was runner-up. Smith's tournament career began to slow down when in 1934 he became head professional at Oakmont Country Club in Glendale, California. He served there until 1946 and died in 1949 at age 59.

Nineteen thirty-two was a wonderful year for Sarazen, and one of his tour victories came when he won the first prize of $1,000 in the True Temper New Orleans Open in that year. In these difficult times, the question of sponsorship was very much a moveable feast. As has been seen elsewhere, sponsorship could often come from a combination of local chambers of commerce and admission and entry fees. However, with the steel shaft now being used more widely, True Temper saw an opportunity to dominate the market. Thus, in addition to the event in New Orleans, the company sponsored spring tournaments in Phoenix, San Antonio and Houston. "True Temper Shafts. *The Choice of Champions*!" was the slogan and Joe Kirkwood, tournament winner and trick shot artist supreme, was one of the firm's signature players. Kirkwood assured golfers that "there is no comparison between steel and hickory shafts." True Temper's investment was rewarded, as it went on to become brand leader. Also of note this year was the fact that Walter Hagen enjoyed two increasingly rare victories at the Western Open and in St. Louis.

As for the year's majors, Olin Dutra won the PGA, the first of his two major titles. The championship was played in September at the Keller Club in Wisconsin and his opponent in the final was Frank Walsh, a somewhat unfancied player, but one who had a number of good finishes on the tour. By the time of the PGA, Dutra was in the middle of a hot streak, as he won both the Chicago and Metropolitan Opens in quick succession, so it was no surprise when he won the 36-hole final by 4/3. Dutra's streak, however, was surpassed that summer by Gene Sarazen, who won not only the British title, but also the U.S. Open. Both were won within the space of a few weeks. In the lead-up to his wins on both sides of the Atlantic, Sarazen provided an insight into what may have helped him. A few weeks before sailing to Britain for what would prove to be the first leg of his double at Prince's in Kent, Sarazen gave an interview to Grantland Rice.

Long before the days of diets and nutritionists, Sarazen confided to

Rice that he was "in training" for the forthcoming championships and that he planned to lose nine pounds by eating only two meals a day. He was also swinging a 30-ounce driver to build up his strength and timing, as well as practicing a range of shots in windy conditions. His strategy clearly worked, as Sarazen won in Britain with a new record total of 283 and closed with a stunning final round of 66 at Fresh Meadow to claim his second National Open title.

One event, which was a footnote to the 1932 season, can retrospectively be seen as a seminal moment in the history of American golf. It marked the professional debut of Byron Nelson and also highlighted the casual approach to "turning pro" which was in evidence at that time. As has been well documented elsewhere, Nelson was introduced to golf when caddying at the Glen Garden club in Texas. As is also well known, another caddie at the time was Ben Hogan. During Nelson's formative years, the pro at Glen Garden was Ted Longworth, who took a keen interest in the young Byron's game. In particular, Longworth advised Nelson to shorten his swing. (Longworth also influenced the young Hogan, particularly in the way he gripped the club.) In November 1932, the Texarkana club, prompted by Longworth, who was now professional there, held a tournament with a total prize fund of $500. By now Nelson had moved on from Glen Garden and was competing in some amateur events. Longworth invited Byron to the Texarkana Open and as an amateur, Nelson made the bus trip to compete. Later Nelson recalled, "It was on that bus trip that I decided to turn pro. When I got there for the qualifying rounds, I asked the tournament officials what I had to do to turn pro, and they told me, 'Pay five dollars and say you're playing for money.' It was as simple as that—no qualifying schools, no mini-tours like they have today."[23] For the record, Nelson finished third and won the significant sum of $75. His mentor, Longworth, won the first prize of $200.

The prelude to 1933 did not look promising—in particular, the western section of the Grapefruit Circuit: "West Coast Winter Golf Hit Hard by Depression"[24] was how one newspaper described the upcoming tournaments in January 1933. Of particular concern was the Los Angeles Open, which usually carried a prize fund of $10,000, but which had now been cut to $5,000. Similarly Agua Caliente, the richest of all, had dropped from a prize fund of $25,000 in 1931 to a purse of $7,500. As a result, it was claimed that certain top players, most of whom were based in Florida, would not travel west, as it was not worth their while. One of these was Sarazen, who quickly went into print and claimed that his winter contract at the Miami Biltmore hotel would not permit him the time to play on the West Coast. As Gene had a reputation for always turning up at big-money events, this did not seem an overly convincing explanation. As it turned out, Sarazen was a late entry in Los Angeles but had to withdraw after 54 holes with illness. In the event, Craig Wood earned $1,525 for winning at Los Angeles, but with a total fund of just under $6,000, the size of the winner's check once again highlighted the uneven distribution of cash prizes.

The mixed nature of purses continued on the east side, with one of the less lucrative events being the Orange Blossom Open at the Lakeland Links in Florida. Here the organizers came up with the novel idea of leaving a box of oranges on each tee. This was not such a bad idea during these times, as a young and broke Ben Hogan once relied on oranges he himself plucked to sustain him during his very harsh introduction to the professional game. With a total fund of only $1,000 and a first prize of $200, it was no surprise that the players were delighted with this bonus.[25] And despite the modest purse, many top players entered, including Hagen, Dutra, Shute and Cooper. As it turned out, the entry fees and gate receipts which were to fund the tournament did not cover the $1,000 purse, so the PGA had to cover the difference. The 36-hole tournament saw Al Watrous claim the last of his eight tour victories. Watrous was twice a Ryder Cup player and was perhaps best known as the man Bobby Jones pipped for the Britsh Open title at Royal Lytham and St. Anne's in 1926. In this event, Jones played a seemingly impossible shot from a fairway bunker on Lytham's daunting 17th hole in the final round.[26]

In many ways, 1933 was the year of Paul Runyan, as he won nine times. Only Snead, Hogan and Nelson won more titles in a single year. Although he tried, Runyan did not get into professional golf via the well-worn caddie route. He was born into a relatively well-off dairy-farming family in Hot Springs, Arkansas, who happened to live across the road from the local golf course. At this time (1918), Hot Springs was one of America's leading gambling centers and attracted celebrities such as Jack Dempsey, Babe Ruth and one Al Capone. Indeed, Runyan forged a life-long friendship with Jack (Greasy Thumbs) Guzick, who handled Capone's financial affairs during the mobster's reign in Chicago. Many of the celebrities who came to Hot Springs for the gambling also liked to play golf and were quite happy to pay handsomely for good caddies or "ball shaggers." This introduction to golf helped Runyan see the commercial possibilities of golf at an early age. As he explained, "I was too small to caddie so I started shagging balls for the club pro. I was thirteen years old and was earning $65 per week so I knew I had to get into the

"Little Poison" Paul Runyan, here flanked by Ben Hogan and Byron Nelson (courtesy USGA).

golf business."[27]

As the sobriquets "Lighthorse" Harry Cooper and "Slammin" Sam Snead suggest, sports writers in the 1930s were fond of nicknames—and "Little Poison" suited Paul Runyan's short game excellence perfectly. The origins of this name may have come from Johnny Revolta when he lost to Runyan in a PGA match. "I outhit him off the tee," Revolta said, "and reached the green before him but once he got the putter in his hand he was poison."[28] If the "poison" referred to his short game, the "little" was because of his size: Runyan stood only 5 feet 7 inches and weighed between 120 and 125 pounds. It was not just his short game which contributed to Runyan's success, but also his mind. After losing to him in the 1939 PGA Championship, Ben Hogan confessed to his wife Valerie,"Runyan knows how to finish a match better than anybody I've ever seen. It's his focus. Paul's concentration is so absolute he doesn't seem to see anything but the next shot. He wasn't the slightest bit intimidated by my drives, He controlled his mind *and* mine." "If I'm going to win," Hogan added, "I've got to be able to do that too."[29]

All told, Runyan won 29 tour events, including PGA titles in 1934 and 1938. He was not shy when it came to assessing his own ability. In a 1978 interview with Al Browning, he rated himself in the top 25 players of all time.[30] Runyan also demonstrated an interest in the technical side of the game at an early stage of his career and his instructional articles were a regular feature in *The American Golfer* during the 1930s. He went on to become a highly regarded teacher, and in later years, Runyan taught Gene Littler and Mickey Wright, among a number of tour players.

Runyan's 1933 season got off to an excellent start when he won at Agua Caliente and took away the $1,500 first prize. In keeping with the tradition of this short-lived event, 23 out of the 56 finishers got paid, with the last prize being $16.66. Moreover, the spring of this year saw Runyan win one of the most unusual tournaments in PGA history. As well as being one of golf's greatest players, Gene Sarazen was one of its most outspoken. One of his more controversial pronouncements was to suggest that the cup size should be enlarged to 8 inches. This, Sarazen argued, would lead to lower scoring for the pros, and make the game more enjoyable for club golfers. The suggestion met with a largely unfavorable response; across the Atlantic, Harry Vardon called it "tommyrot."[31] However, as a form of compromise and in an attempt to create some much needed publicity, Miami hosted the FLOG tournament in March 1933, with the cup size being 6 inches in diameter, and not the usual 4.25 inches. (FLOG was "golf" spelled backward.) Being an excellent putter and the man in form, it was no surprise that Runyan won the handsome $1,000 first prize, with a score of 266—18 under par.

In the following weeks, the money was more modest, with Craig Wood winning the $300 first prize at Radium Springs and Runyan winning a similar amount when taking the Virginia Beach Open. However, at the end of March, the prestigious North and South tournament was held in the affluent location of Pinehurst, which liked to advertise itself as the place where "There ain't no Depression." The resort even had its own newspaper to underline this image: as well as the latest golf news, advertisements for the evening cocktail hour adorned the front page of *The Daily Press*. However, despite the "no Depression" billing, on the eve of the North and South tournament, there was a reminder of these harsh times when an exhibition was held to raise funds for unemployed professionals. The match was organized by former National Open champion Johnny Farrell and featured an unusual "fiveball" of Hagen, Sarazen, Armour, Runyan and Craig Wood.

It was no surprise that the exhibition was planned by Farrell. Words such as "classy" and "gentleman" were often used to describe him by both fellow players and journalists. Coming from a poor, immigrant Irish family, Farrell rose to the top of his profession both as a player and as a club professional, notably at the Baltusrol Club, New Jersey, where he served from 1934 until 1972. After he retired, Baltusrol made him an honorary member and even named a room in the clubhouse in his honor.

Apart from his win at the U.S. Open in 1927 (he defeated Jones in a 36-hole play-off), Farrell won seven tournaments out of eight consecutive starts in the same year. Farrell's personality and his standing in the game made him an ideal figure to promote the "fiveball" venture. The fund-raiser at Pinehurst was a success, with large galleries turning out and a total of $1,000 being raised. As for the main event, Joe Kirkwood won the very handsome first prize of $1,200, with Harry Cooper collecting $800 as runner-up.

Nineteen thirty-three was a significant year for Kirkwood, as the North and South tournament and the Canadian Open, which he won later in the year, represented his final victories on tour. The Australian-born Kirkwood was undoubtedly better known as the world's leading trick shot artist as well as for his global exhibition tours with Sarazen and more especially Hagen. In the 12 months preceding the North and South, it was estimated that Joe had traveled 60,000 miles and played 180 different courses. With typical flourish, Grantland Rice summed up his travels as follows: "Through the last year or so he has chased the bounding pellet through Japan, Manchuria, parts of China, Australia, Hawaii, England, Scotland and France."[32] Later, in 1934, Kirkwood and Sarazen embarked on an exhibition tour which included stops in the Caribbean, Central and South America, Fiji and Samoa. Exhibitions were a serious source of income in the 1930s. The handsome Kirkwood suffered somewhat from his image as an entertainer and showman, as it often camouflaged the fact that he was a fine golfer, who came tantalizingly close on at least two occasions to winning the British Open and who won 18 tour events.

The two domestic majors of 1933 were won by Johnny Goodman, who won the U.S. Open, and Gene Sarazen, who won the PGA title. Goodman's victory was especially noteworthy because he was an amateur—the last to win the title. Since Jones's retirement in 1930, the professionals had enjoyed something of a respite from amateurs embarrassing them in the National Open—at least until 1933 and Johnny Goodman. Ralph Guldahl had a 4-foot putt on the final green to earn a tie and perhaps preserve the honor of his fellow pros, but he missed.

Goodman's win was also unusual in another way. History suggests that many of the leading amateurs in America tended to come from comfortable backgrounds. While Francis Ouimet started his golfing life as a caddie in Boston, the leaders in the nonpaid ranks were more likely to be found in the families which produced Bobby Jones and Jerry Travers, who in the second decade of the century won both the National Professional and Amateur Championships. Goodman, however, seemed to defy all the norms in this regard. After his stunning win at North Shore, Chicago, one headline read "He Used to Caddie, Play with Borrowed Sticks, Ride the Cattle Cars, But Now Look at Johnny Goodman."[33] The newspaper did not exaggerate. Goodman, from Lithuanian/English heritage, was one of 10 children whose mother died when he was 11 years old. He also came from the "packing district" of his native Omaha. Furthermore, while Jones learned the game in Atlanta from Stewart Maiden and Jerry Travers was taught by another Scot, National Open winner Alex Smith, Goodman never had a formal golf lesson. He learned by caddying and observing. Notwithstanding these apparent disadvantages, Goodman forged a fine amateur career before 1933, which included being runner-up in the National Amateur the year before. And one thing Goodman did not lack was confidence. In the aftermath of his victory he claimed, "Sure, I expected to win. I didn't come down here for the fun of it. All I did was get in there and pitch."[34] Johnny did not turn professional and cash in on his success, but instead went on to win many titles, including the National Amateur in 1937. However, many years later he did become a professional and enjoyed a teaching career for roughly 10 years before his premature death in 1970 at age 60.

The PGA Championship of 1933 was also noteworthy as—not for the only time during this decade—the tournament highlighted the internal wrangling within the Association. Usually the tournament was held in September or October, but this led to some complaints from players that this did not leave the winner enough time to cash in on his success. Ideally, it was argued, an earlier date would leave time for a series of lucrative exhibitions before the Grapefruit Circuit picked up again in December. So in 1933, the holding of the PGA's flagship event in August seemed to offer the players an ideal solution. However, as we shall see later, 1933 was a Ryder Cup "away year," which also meant a strong U.S. entry in the British Open. The result was that on returning from Britain, many players, including Hagen, Wood, Sarazen and Shute, told the PGA they would not contest the Championship in Wisconsin, but instead preferred to play in some prearranged exhibitions. Shute especially stood to make a considerable sum as the new British Open winner.

The response was strong, with the PGA suggesting that the players who did compete would play only for the trophy and whatever money came from gate receipts. There would be no official prize fund. Tommy Armour was the most vociferous of the critics and leveled particularly stinging words at his old adversaries and friends Hagen and Sarazen, whom he suggested were in any event "washed up." He exempted Shute to some degree, suggesting he was entitled to "cash in," but the rest, he stated, were biting the hand that fed them. As it turned out, Sarazen entered late and was deemed the man who saved the PGA Championship of 1933. He also won his third PGA title with victory in the final over Willie Goggin. After his win, he said with his usual bite that the result was not bad for a "washed up" golfer.[35]

The aforementioned 1933 Ryder Cup matches were held in Southport, England. A certain amount of controversy surrounded the original make-up of the American team, notably in regard to the omission of 1931 National Open winner, Billy Burke. During the early 1930s, the team was selected on the basis of votes cast for individual players by both national and regional PGA committees. Gaining a place on the team was regarded as prestigious, so competition was keen. In the event, Burke was selected, as a place was left open for the winner of the U.S. Open of 1933, who turned out to be amateur Johnny Goodman. As Goodman was ineligible, Burke was given a place. There were also reports that not all was well between Hagen and Sarazen, with Sarazen feeling that as winner of the U.S. and British Opens the previous year, he, and not Hagen, should have the honor of captaining the team. Notwithstanding these distractions, the U.S. team went into the match as favorites. Britain, having clearly learned some lessons from the 1931 matches, won the match by six and a half points to five and a half. The contest came down to the 36th hole of the singles match between Denny Shute and Syd Easterbrook. Shute three putted and the Cup returned to Britain. The response in Britain was one of great joy but in some sections of the American press, there was a somewhat patronizing reaction, as evidenced by syndicated journalist Francis J. Powers. "The British professionals," he wrote, "may appear duffers when playing in this country or even in their own Open Championship, but at match-play over an English course, they appear to have the numbers of our stars."[36] To be fair to Powers, he did go on to suggest that the British victory would be good for the game of golf and for the Ryder Cup.

As was the tradition, the American team went on to play in the Open Championship being held that year at St. Andrews. Included in the U.S. challengers for the Open were Hagen (the team captain), Sarazen, Smith, Dutra, and Runyan. Here, Shute more than compensated for his disappointment at Southport by defeating another team member, Craig Wood, in a 36-hole play-off.

As British Open champion, Shute also earned the right to compete with Johnny Goodman for the unofficial "World Championship of Golf." This event was the brainchild of Henry L. Doherty, a multimillionaire oil man who owned several hotels and country clubs, many of which were in Florida. Doherty was also a man with political connections and was chairman of the national committee charged with organizing countrywide "birthday balls" to celebrate FDR's 52nd birthday, which fell on January 30, 1934. The main purpose of this initiative was to raise funds for the Georgia Warm Springs Foundation. Georgia Springs was the spa where Roosevelt recovered from polio and which he subsequently bought. Even in these difficult times, it was reported that the nation was responding to Doherty's request with donations totaling $1 million.[37] Doherty, who saw sports as the ideal vehicle for promoting both the state and his hotels, sponsored events in both show-jumping and swimming. Golf, however, was Doherty's biggest draw. As owner of the prestigious Miami Biltmore, he sponsored one of the more lucrative winter tournaments, which bore the hotel's name. Thus a "World Championship" was not an altogether surprising development. The match would be between the reigning U.S. and British Open golf champions and the winner would receive a very handsome gold cup bearing Doherty's name. In fact, the Doherty Gold Cup was first played for the previous year between Gene Sarazen and Olin Dutra. Dutra's inclusion was due to the fact that in 1932, Sarazen won the Open Championships of Britain and America; as PGA champion, Olin was therefore invited to play. Sarazen won the 72-hole match by 11 and 10. The local press drummed up publicity for

Doherty and his trophy by producing banner headlines which omitted the word "unofficial" but instead proclaimed "Sarazen Wins World Golf Title."[38] The 1933 event was a much closer affair, with Shute defending the honor of the professionals by defeating amateur Goodman on the last hole of their 72-hole contest.

In December 1933, effectively the start of the 1934 season, at age

Willie MacFarlane, one of the many Scotsmen who came to America, and his dog (courtesy USGA).

42, Willie MacFarlane achieved one of the final victories in what had been a wonderful career, when he captured the Miami Biltmore Open and the sizeable first prize of $2,500. MacFarlane learned his golf in his native Aberdeen, Scotland, before emigrating to America. In total he had 21 tournament victories. However, what distinguished his career was his win in the 1925 U.S. Open, when he defeated Bobby Jones in a play-off.

Nineteen thirty-four followed a predictable pattern, with many tournaments offering total purses of between $1,500 and $2,500. There were some exceptions, such as the always lucrative Agua Caliente Open won by Wiffy Cox. Cox collected $1,500, but as was the tradition in Tijuana, this left the sizeable sum of $6,500 for the rest of the prize winners. There was also the $5,500 Los Angeles Open, for which MacDonald Smith received $1,375 as the winner. Later on that year, Horton Smith earned $1,000 for winning at Louisville. This event was sponsored by local sports equipment firm Hillerich and Bradsby, which produced the PowerBilt range of clubs endorsed by Olin Dutra. Surprisingly, this was one of the rare occasions when a leading club manufacturer entered the sponsorship field and availed of what seemed like an excellent opportunity to gain some publicity for its products.

As we know, equipment manufacturers such as Spalding helped subsidize Fred Corcoran's salary, but it is clear that shaft maker True Temper's sponsorship of a number of events benefited the firm considerably. Given that fact, it may seem surprising that more club and ball makers did not follow suit. It appears, however, that manufacturers thought the best form of marketing was the practice of having a star name promoting your equipment—and the leading manufacturers were very active in this regard. For example, Gene Sarazen, Sam Snead, Ralph Guldahl, and Johnny Revolta played Wilson; Tommy Armour represented MacGregor; Henry Picard and Craig Wood played Dunlop; Olin Dutra and Vic Ghezzi were with Powerbilt; and for much of the period, Byron Nelson played Spalding before he signed with MacGregor toward the end of the decade. Retainers for the players were not substantial and the real money came from win bonuses. For example, when Byron Nelson won the prestigious Western Open in 1939, his first prize was $750. However, Spalding gave him a $500 bonus. As with almost everything in this decade, results were the only guarantee of financial security.

Nineteen thirty-four, however, gained a special place in golf history, as it saw the inaugural holding of the Masters. At the start, Bobby Jones did not care for the name "Masters," as he felt it was too presumptuous.

Inaugural Masters winner Horton Smith shows his style in a bunker (courtesy Tufts Archives, Pinehurst, North Carolina).

In fact, the event was originally known as the Augusta National Invitation Tournament, but some journalists had already included the name "Masters" in their reports. Regardless of its title, the tournament has always been accorded major status. The tournament was invitation only and apart from Sarazen, who was on an exhibition tour in South America, all of the top players were in the 60-man field. But what elevated the tournament from being just another stop on the Grapefruit Circuit was the presence of Jones. Apart from both the course and the event being inspired by him, the fact that he was making his competitive "comeback" brought a great deal of publicity to the tournament. Many of the pre-tournament headlines unsurprisingly suggested that Jones's return would once again strike fear into the hearts of the pros. Associated Press reporter Alan Gould, for example, claimed that the professionals approached Augusta more in hope than in expectation at the prospect of taking on Bobby "in his own backyard."[39] Walter Hagen, however, advised caution, expressing the view that a four-year lay-off from competitive golf might prove difficult, even for Jones. As it turned out, Jones finished down the field on 294. Honest as ever, Bobby admitted that, in a manner similar to Vardon before him, his putting had gone. "I experienced something bordering the jitters every time I stepped up to one of them," was how he described his fear of short putts.[40] Jones continued to compete in the Masters but many years later he would admit that his experiences at Augusta in 1934 convinced him that he "simply had not the desire nor the willingness to take the punishment necessary to compete in that kind of company."[41]

The winner of the first Masters was Horton Smith, with a score of 284. Smith was yet one more player on whom the golf writers conferred a nickname. In his case it was "the Joplin Ghost," as in Joplin, Missouri (Smith's home state). Smith, one of the more cerebral professionals, was very interested in tour politics and indeed served on the PGA tournament committee during his illustrious career. Smith was ideally suited to this role, as in his own playing capacity, he was fastidious in writing thank-you letters to host clubs and tournament sponsors. Tommy Armour said of him that "his manners and general conduct are so completely correct that Emily Post could have written about him as exhibit A in her book on etiquette."[42] Later, in the 1950s, he was elected president of the PGA for three consecutive years.

Smith also displayed a degree of independence when he deviated from the traditional path of using a major victory to increase his "worth" as a club professional. For example, he was head professional at the prestigious Oak Park Country Club, Illinois, when he won his first Masters title. Smith's retainer was worth $3,000 per year. However, as noted in Chapter 1, Smith became heavily involved in promoting Spalding equipment and in 1935 he resigned from Oak Park to devote more time to Spalding as well as playing the tour. His parting from Oak Park was amicable, with the Masters winner being made an honorary member, which in the 1930s was considered quite an honor for a professional golfer. Interestingly, Smith was replaced by his brother, Ren, whose salary was half of Horton's.

But most of all, Horton Smith was an exceptional player and regarded as one of the greatest ever putters. He made one of the most impressive entrances into professional golf when, in his freshman year of 1929, he had seven victories and amassed a total of $14,000 in prize money. In total, Smith won 32 tour events and played on five Ryder Cup teams. Smith also became a teacher of note, with Tony Lema being among those to benefit from his wisdom.

Another major winner in 1934 was Olin Dutra in the U.S. Open at Merion. Dutra was a Latin American who followed Gene Sarazen's example and made the grade in professional golf. Dutra hailed from California and was of Spanish ancestry. He was also a member of the "golfing brothers" fraternity, which was prevalent in America, such as the seven Turnesas and Ray and Lloyd Mangrum. Olin's brother Mortie also played the circuit with some distinction. Olin Dutra was a large man whose resembled boxer Jack Dempsey in looks but "who handled his putter like an elephant with a teaspoon."[43]

In the 1934 event Dutra gained some extra publicity as the "Sick Man at Merion."[44] In an early example of the maxim "Beware the ailing golfer," he won although suffering from dysentery throughout the tournament. Dutra lost several pounds during the week and took tablets regularly. However, this publicity should not camouflage one of the greatest comebacks in U.S. Open history. At this time (and up to 1964, when Ken Venturi won

The Californian, Olin Dutra, with the 1934 U.S. Open trophy (courtesy Wilshire Country Club).

at Congressional), the last day consisted of 36 holes. Going into "Open Saturday," Dutra lay a full eight shots behind Bobby Cruickshank and five shots behind the man who would ultimately finish second, Gene Sarazen. Comebacks were not unknown to Dutra. In the previous year's Open Championship at St. Andrews, he lay a full 12 shots back after 36 holes, yet missed out by only one on a play-off with Denny Shute and Craig Wood. Ultimately the 1934 U.S. Open was decided on the final nine holes, which were vividly described by George Trevor in *Golf Illustrated* magazine.

Golf Illustrated was very much an amateur-centered publication, as might be expected from its owner, the noted course designer and highly conservative A.W. Tillinghast. The Cuban Amateur Championship, for example, was deemed more worthy of space than a regular stop on the Grapefruit Circuit. However, the U.S. Open was a "must" for all golf publications and reports usually came from George Trevor, who was a golf writer of considerable standing during this period. It was Trevor who was credited with coining the phrase "the Impregnable Quadrilateral of Golf" to describe Bobby Jones' Grand Slam of 1930.

Trevor enjoyed writing with a flourish and his pieces regularly contained Shakespearean references. For his report of Dutra's victory, Trevor was given the prominent position of page 10 in *Golf Illustrated,* and his description covered three pages. As well as Dutra's success, Trevor's article devoted a great deal of space to Sarazen's problems on the last nine holes of the championship. During this stretch, Sarazen lost a three-shot lead, notably because of a seven at the par four 11th hole. In keeping with his style (and the magazine's cultured ethos), Trevor used the image of a Shakespearean tragedy as a metaphor for Sarazen's woes; he also quoted the distinguished French military strategist Marshal Ferdinand Foch, who believed that "battles are lost in the minds of those who fight them."[45] This was in reference to what Trevor believed to be Sarazen's somewhat dispirited closing holes. In the end, Dutra won by one by compiling rounds of 71 and 72 in windy conditions on one of America's toughest tests. His total score was 293.

With the British Open being played a few weeks later, Dutra may have been expected to try and complete the "double," especially after his fine showing in 1933. However, immediately after Merion, Dutra declared what his priorities were and announced that instead he would go on an exhibition tour with crowd puller, Walter Hagen. Dutra admitted that he had failed to cash in on his PGA win two years earlier and had no intention of missing out this time.

During his illustrious career, Dutra won 19 tour events as well as his two majors. He was also a Ryder Cup player. What was also notable about Dutra, however, was that not long after his second major title, he took a job as head professional at the Wilshire Country Club, Los Angeles, and made increasingly few tournament appearances. In doing so, Dutra highlighted a feature of golf at this time: leading tournament players (even major winners) wanting and needing the security of a good club job.

In Olin Dutra's case he was the ideal head professional for Wilshire. He was a local man and had played in the Los Angeles Open at Wilshire on a few occasions. He also won the California PGA title six times. Thus, as well as being nationally (and internationally) known, he had acquired a great deal of local status. During the remainder of the Depression years, Dutra spent most of his time teaching the members at Wilshire but when important events such as the U.S. Open came along, he competed. To do this, he had to receive permission from the Wilshire committee. All in all he stayed at Wilshire until 1945, being paid what the club referred to as a "modest salary."[46] In the late 1940s, Olin crossed the border into Mexico, where he spent some time as national director of golf in an attempt to develop the game locally.

The PGA title went to Paul Runyan, in what was a rehearsal of his win over Snead in 1938, as his vanquished opponent in the final was the long-hitting Craig Wood. Again, the scribes were not short of nicknames for him. "The Blonde Bomber," "the Adonis of the Fairways," and "No. 1 Wood" were three which captured both his handsome features and his driving prowess. When it came to length, Wood ranked with the acknowledged power hitters of the day, Lawson Little and Jimmy Thomson. Throughout this decade, Wood seemed destined to end his career in a similar fashion to Harry Cooper, without a major title. In all, Wood lost three play-offs in the 1930s: to Denny Shute in the 1933 Open at St. Andrews; to Sarazen in the 1935 Masters; and to Nelson in the 1939 U.S. Open. Wood eventually had his day in 1941, when he won both the Masters and the U.S. Open. In total, he won 21 tour events and played three times on the Ryder Cup team. Wood hailed from Lake Placid, New York, and in 1954, he received the unique honor of having the Lake Placid Golf and Country Club change its name to the Craig Wood Golf Course. In so many ways this honor symbolized the development of professional golf in America, as Wood had caddied at Lake Placid as a boy.

The David and Goliath clash between Runyan and Wood was food and drink for the journalists and once again, George Trevor led the way with his report in *Golf Illustrated*. The match, played at Buffalo, produced one of the Championship's most thrilling finishes, with the pint-sized Runyan defeating his long-hitting opponent at the 38th hole. The drama and color of the match were eloquently captured by Trevor, never more so than in his description of the 36th hole. Here he noted how "The ample theatre fronting the clubhouse was gay with spectators—streamlined girls in bright chiffons, mere males in shirt sleeves—as the finalists hove in sight, like twin crusaders leading a raucous army to the assaults."[47] In the event, both "crusaders" holed medium-length putts to ensure the match continued, before Runyan got down in two from 80 yards to win the title at the 38th hole. By then Trevor had decided that Runyan's recoveries did not belong "in the category of golf shots ... rather did they savor of black magic."[48] And to make sure that his readers were in no doubt as to the difference in style and power of the two finalists, Trevor made numerous references to this fact. "It is human nature to root for David against Goliath.... Pop gun had conquered howitzer ... a wispy St. George taming a fire-spewing dragon."[49]

Trevor also included some analysis of technique in his report, notably in regard to Runyan whom, he claimed, "at impact he pulls his left foot out of line and otherwise violates the canons of good form, proving that a genius can scoff at copy-book rules." The more elegant Wood, in contrast, could hit his drives 280 yards with a brassie (a no. 2 wood). This, according to the player himself, was because he teed the ball high and struck it "on the upswing, hitting it up and over to insure a long carry, plus a good roll."[50] This was just one more way for Trevor to convey to his reader the contrast between the maverick Runyan and the "Apollo-like" Wood.

One other incident of note in 1934 concerned Joe Turnesa, of *the* golfing "band of brothers." In total there were seven golfing brothers, six of whom were professionals. Like other players of Italian origin, such as Sarazen and Manero, the Turnesa's learned the game as caddies. In their case, it was at the Fairview Country Club, where their father Vitale served for 54 years, mostly as a greenkeeper. Interestingly, and in a sign of these harsh times, the six professional Turnesa's insisted that the remaining sibling Willie stay an amateur so he could have some of the advantages they never had, such as a proper education. Indeed, the older brothers helped put Willie through college. Their support was vindicated as Willie twice won the U.S. Amateur, as well as the British title.

Joe was undoubtedly the best golfer in the family. Twice a Ryder Cup player, he was pipped by one to the National Open crown by Jones in 1926; in 1927, Hagen also beat him on the 36th hole in the final of the PGA. However, in the 1930s, Turnesa experienced the yips. In the days long before the broom-handle or belly putter, he found a novel way to solve his putting problems. Putting with his right hand only, Turnesa won the Long Island Open with a "sawn-off" putter, which he used only 29 times in the first round. As *The Evening Independent* put it, this was definitely a case of not letting "the left hand know what the right is doing."[51] Eventually, Turnesa gave up this method, citing being pestered by golfers wanting advice on one-handed putting as the main reason. This year also saw the emergence of three-time Masters champion-to-be, Jimmy Demaret, who won the domestic Texas PGA title.

As we saw earlier, the Grapefruit Circuit included a regular trip across the border to Canada for the Canadian Open. However, 1935 saw the brief emergence of a tournament which had significant implications both for the tour and for professional golf in Canada: the General Brock Open. At this time, Canada was also heavily affected by the Great Depression, notably by the Smoot-Hawley Act, which saw Washington legislators place penal tariffs on imports from Canada into the United States. The loss of farm goods' exports, a vital part of Canada's economy, was a particular blow and cost thousands of jobs. However, professional golf survived and one important sponsor saw the game as a way of attracting publicity. The sponsor concerned was Vernon G. Cardy, who owned a chain of hotels including the Royal in Montreal and the Prince Edward in Windsor. When he bought the General Brock Hotel near Niagara Falls, it was widely known that the hotel was a loss maker. Cardy, a keen golfer, saw hosting a tournament as the best way to boost the image of his hotel. He was the first commercial sponsor of golf in Canada. Furthermore, having put some of his own money up, he managed to persuade distilling giant Seagram to co-sponsor the event. This was a seminal moment in professional golf in Canada as the Royal Canadian Golf Association (RCGA), which had sponsored the Canadian Open since 1904, was so impressed with the General Brock Open that the following year Seagram took over sponsoring the national championship, beginning with a $5,000 purse in 1936. This arrangement lasted until 1970, with the winner in the intervening years receiving the famous Seagram Gold Cup. Meanwhile, the General Brock tournament itself had a short life, as 1937 saw its final staging. Nevertheless, Cardy and his hotel are still recognized for their contribution to the development of the professional game in Canada. As for the 1935 event, the tournament was played at the Lookout Point course about 12 miles from the General Brock Hotel and the winner was Tony Manero with a score of 291, five under par. The first prize was $750.

Nineteen thirty-five also saw Vic Ghezzi achieve his first tour victory, when he won the Los Angeles Open in January and a prize of $1,350. A tall New Jersey native, Ghezzi was one of the increasing number of professionals from Italian stock. He would go on to win 11 times on tour. One of these was the Hershey fourball of 1938, where Ghezzi contributed to a little slice of golfing history: his partner at Hershey was Ben Hogan and this was Hogan's first tour win. Ghezzi would also win the PGA title in 1941, when he beat Nelson in the final at Cherry Hills.

In general, 1935 was a relatively lean year financially; however, there were some large first prizes, such as Henry Picard's $2,000 for winning the Atlanta Metropolitan Open in April. Picard was another joy to the golf writers, who at different times dubbed him "the Hershey Hurricane," "the Candy Kid" and "the Chocolate Soldier." The first of these nicknames referred to his home club of Hershey, and the latter two to the obvious association with Hershey's most famous product—chocolate. Indeed, apart from his win in Atlanta, 1935 was a significant one for Picard, as it was the year he was offered a contract by the Hershey Country Club.

When Picard emerged as a serious tournament player, he set a new course record of 67 at the Hershey Open in 1934. Those at the Hershey Country Club were so impressed that they offered him a retainer to represent the club on tour and to look after the club and its members during the rest of the year. The club were so delighted with their "capture" that a dinner dance to welcome Picard was held in April 1935. Looking after the members was no small task. Picard was an excellent and enthusiastic teacher and as there were four courses at Hershey under his charge, he was a busy man when not playing tournaments.

Picard was undoubtedly well suited to the twin strands of his professional career, but he was also fortunate that chocolate magnate and philanthropist Milton Hershey financed his arrangement with the club. In a deal seemingly on a different level to that of Olin Dutra's at Wilshire, Picard's contract was worth $5,000 per year—very good money in the 1930s; as a bonus on top of that, Milton Hershey matched Picard's tour earnings, dollar for dollar. Picard's deal also included a home for himself and his family. He combined his wonderful playing career with tending to his members at Hershey until 1941, when he moved on and recommended that Ben Hogan take his place. However, Hogan did not receive the "dollar for dollar" bonus of his predecessor.

In a decade when Nelson and Snead first came to prominence, Picard was acknowledged by his peers as being a supreme long iron player, with the no. 2 being his speciality. Picard gained additional fame for supplying Sam Snead with the driver he used for most of his victories and for offering to finance a young Ben Hogan when the champion-to-be was at a low ebb in his career. Regarding his offering help for Hogan, Picard was typically modest. As he explained to Al Barkow, "One night while on the way to the coast I stopped at the Blackstone Hotel to have dinner.... I look over at a corner of the dining room and Hogan was over there with his wife and they were arguing. I didn't know Hogan real well then, but I walk over and say. 'What are you arguing about?' She said she wanted Ben to go to the coast, but they couldn't afford to. I looked at him and said, "I'm not the richest man in the world, but if you need money, I've got it. You go to the coast with her.'"[52] Hogan did not need to avail of this offer but he never forgot Picard's generosity and dedicated his first book to him. In fact, Hogan's dedication went further than the usual format as he said that "Picard by his offers of financial assistance, his recommendations, words of encouragement and golfing hints, has helped me more than I can ever repay."[53] Regardless of these caveats, Picard's record stands on its own, as he was a golfer of the highest class with 26 tournament victories and the 1938 Masters and 1939 PGA titles. His best year was 1939, when he won five other titles apart from the PGA. He also made four Ryder Cup appearances.

This was also the year when Harold "Jug" McSpaden announced himself with victories at Pasadena, Sacramento and the San Francisco Match-Play Open. For once, the nickname "Jug" was not donated by the game's journalists. McSpaden himself could not recall when or why he got the name. Hailing from Kansas, he learned the game as a caddie. As a very young man, he saw Vardon and Ray play an exhibition at the Mission Hills Country Club. When he became a professional, McSpaden was a long, wild hitter, and was even dubbed "an in and outer" by way of describing his erratic performances. However, after some advice from Hagen, he shortened his swing and went on to become an impressive player who would win 17 official PGA events. More than half of these victories came during the Depression years. McSpaden also lost to Denny Shute in the final of the 1937 PGA Championship, having been two up with three to play in the 36-hole final. This was the closest he would come to winning a major title.

The following decade saw McSpaden gain considerable fame as one half of "the Gold-Dust Twins," the name given to himself and Nelson as testimony to their friendship and their ability to win money, notably during Nelson's streak of 1945. During this year, McSpaden finished second 13 times.

Nineteen thirty-five also featured one of the circuit's more exotic trips: the British Colonial tournament in Nassau, the Bahamas. Nassau had hosted a tournament for the pros back in 1928, but had dropped out after the crash. However, in recent years and in an attempt to boost golf in the Bahamas, it had made a comeback, with a decent prize fund of $5,000 and—of equal importance—subsidized expenses for the professionals. For example, a round-trip cruise fare which included the entrance fee came to $24.50, with a $1.50 per day European hotel plan. In this instance, the relatively unknown Leo Mallory from Connecticut won the first prize of $1,000 by one shot over Johnny Revolta.

However, 1935 is perhaps best remembered as the year that the Masters came to public prominence. As noted earlier, the tournament did not generate a huge deal of publicity in its inaugural year, but if the newspapers were somewhat sparing in their coverage, golf lovers were more than compensated by O.B. Keeler's report in *The American Golfer*. Apart from *Golf Illustrated*, *The American Golfer* was the other main golfing journal of this era and had the distinct advantage of being edited by the prolific Grantland Rice. In fact, the magazine started in 1907 and was originally edited by the multiple U.S. Amateur champion, Walter Travis. Rice remained in this position until 1936, when the journal merged with *Sports Illustrated*. The magazine also had Bobby Jones as its managing editor and Glenna Collett Vare as an associate editor. Having two of America's greatest ever golfers on its board *and* writing articles did no harm to the publication's image. Nor was it disadvantaged by the fact that Jones's biographer and good friend Keeler was a regular contributor.

Keeler was born in Chicago but his family moved to Georgia when he was four and his southern identity was never in doubt. In his early days of journalism he covered crime, among other stories, but it was as sports editor of *The Atlanta Journal* that he found his true niche. His involvement with sport's and golf in particular brought him into the world of Bobby Jones and their friendship was perhaps unmatched in the game's history. In total, Keeler watched (and reported on) Jones in 27 national championships. The pair often roomed together. Later Jones would write, "I never felt so lonely as on a golf course in the midst of a championship with thousands of people around, especially when things started to go wrong and crowds started wandering away. It was then that

I began to look around for Keeler and I always found him."[54] As a member of golf's literary establishment, Keeler was certainly a "catch" for the magazine. On occasions, the journal also featured articles by Bernard Darwin, usually on golfing news from Britain. Combined, this was certainly a team of golfing heavyweights.

The American Golfer had certain similarities with *Golf Illustrated,* in that it leaned heavily on instructional articles, amateur golf and many columns promoting Florida especially as an ideal golfing location. However, unlike its rival, when it did report on tour events, *The American Golfer* did so in a much more thorough fashion.

This was certainly true of the 1935 Masters. By this time, the word "Masters" was being used more frequently. Keeler began his thorough report with a quote from the resident Augusta professional, Ed Dudley. Speaking after the event, Dudley said, "Well, I think everything happened in this tournament that ever happened in any other tournament that ever was."[55] Dudley may have been guilty of some exaggeration but not much, as this Masters is generally regarded as the one that turned the event into the fourth major. It ended in a tie between Craig Wood and Sarazen (Gene won the 36-hole play-off), but it was the finish in regulation play which became such a part of golfing lore.

Before getting to that, however, Keeler took care to report on the preceding days, the weather, the quality of the field, and the performance of host Bobby Jones.[56] He also introduced, to this writer at least, a new phrase from the golfing lexicon when recounting Ed Dudley's second round as starting with a "buzzard five."[57] This neat and colorful term seemed to be a perfect way of describing a bogey, as opposed to the birdie and eagle which followed later. The numbers who saw Sarazen play the 15th hole have long been a matter of contention, with some suggesting that there were only a handful present as opposed to the hundreds who claim to have been there. However, there is no doubt that for the climax, Keeler was in the advantageous position of walking with Sarazen.

Put simply, Craig Wood birdied the last hole. While playing the 14th hole and on hearing this news, Sarazen's partner Hagen said, "Well, Gene, that looks as if it's all over." According to the watching Keeler, "Gene's square brown face was set in the bulldog look he wears when the clutch is on." "Oh, I don't know," said Sarazen. "They might go in from anywhere."[58] These words, witnessed by Keeler, may go down as the most prophetic in the game, for as the whole golfing world knows, Sarazen holed his fairway wood shot at the par five 15th hole for what was—and maybe remains—the most famous single shot in golf. Interestingly, Keeler described the club Sarazen used as a no. 4 spoon (for many, a spoon was a 3 wood) and suggested that should the winner ever think of devising a family coat of arms, it should feature the famous club "rampant as a crest."[59]

Keeler's report of this historic moment was a mixture of the wonderfully vivid, as in his description of the crowd's reaction when the famous shot found the bottom of the hole—"and then the tornado broke"[60]—and just the right amount of quotes. This combination, in a manner similar to Rice, gave the lucky readers the sense of "being there."

In later years, the Masters committee was reluctant to publish the amount of prize money won by the players, as it was deemed to be somewhat vulgar. But in these early days there were no restrictions: Sarazen's winner's check was the very handsome sum of $1,500. However, the traditional prize fund pattern applied, with 12th-place Johnny Revolta winning just $50.

The U.S. Open that year at Oakmont was won by Sam Parks, Jr. The club had already hosted two U.S. Amateur Championships, the most recent of which saw Bobby Jones lift the trophy in 1925. However, this was the first time the National Open was held at the penal Pittsburgh course, with its famous "church pews" fairway bunker. Oakmont regularly rivaled Pine Valley as being the toughest of all courses in the United States. The severity of the examination was summed up by Grantland Rice: "Oakmont with its ghost-like, haunted greens peering out into the fairways, is something more than a savage test of golf. It is also the type of course that breaks down the mental side and rips into the nerves."[61] In a

Sam Parks, Jr., the surprise but worthy winner of the 1935 U.S. Open (courtesy USGA).

tournament which has specialized in surprise winners such as Jack Fleck and Orville Moody, Parks was probably the "darkest of all the dark horses"[62] to have won. And it was not just Parks's win which was unusual: the player himself was somewhat different from his fellow professionals. For example, in contrast to the many ex-caddies who rose to the top of the professional game, Parks learned the game as a member of the Highland Country Club in his native Pittsburgh. Highland was a country club in every sense, and it regularly featured on the social pages as well as the sports columns. As a 13-year-old, Sam had the good fortune to receive lessons from Gene Sarazen, who was professional there in his formative golfing years. Interestingly, Sarazen advised Sam to stay with the Vardon grip and not the interlocking model so favored by his teacher. Parks went on to Pittsburgh University, where he captained the golf team.

Parks may have also been unusual in the professional ranks in that he neither drank nor smoked. He was a man who possessed a calm and

Johnny Revolta, the master bunker player (courtesy USGA).

measured temperament and it was recorded that "his language, even in the wake of a missed two-foot putt, would become a missionary."[63] Sam's calm temperament and measured approach were instrumental in his 1935 victory. Named "Methodical Sam" by Grantland Rice, he plotted his way around the brutal Oakmont course, and with his score of 299, he was the only player to break 300 for the championship. Rice also concluded that "head, heart, course knowledge and an unhurried swing carried Sam Parks through to the top."[64] It also helped that Oakmont, being near Pittsburgh, was a "local" course for Parks and one he practiced on regularly in the weeks before the event. After his win Parks was selected for the Ryder Cup team, but he never won another tournament of note.

The PGA title that year went to Johnny Revolta, who defeated Tommy Armour in the final of the PGA Championship. When he arrived on the tournament scene, Revolta was described as being "tall, raw boned with great locks of shaggy black hair."[65] Later in his career, his looks were likened to Abe Lincoln's. Like Tommy Armour, Revolta had powerful hands, which he believed were the result of hours spent behind the plow as a boy. One of a growing number of Italian American golfers, such as Tony Manero and Toney Penna, Revolta openly expressed his admiration for Sarazen as the "first of our clan to become one of golf's greats."[66] A self-taught player, Revolta won 18 tour events during his career. Fourballs, notably the Miami International, were big business during this decade and from 1935 to 1937, Revolta won this event three years running with Henry Picard.

Revolta also gained recognition because of his association with the sand wedge. Today, we are used to players carrying three or even four wedges, but Revolta was ahead of his time in this regard. He regularly carried three sand irons: one for soft sand, one for hard sand and the rough, and one to use from the fairway when he needed to stop his ball quickly. He was an acknowledged master in this department of the game and wedges bearing his name were popular for many years.

The PGA championship was played at the Twin Hills club in Oklahoma, a state which for many holds a special place in the imagination when it comes to thoughts or discussions of the Great Depression. Words such as "Okie" and "Dustbowl," for instance, were and remain synonymous with the poverty and humiliation endured by many of the state's inhabitants during this decade. For a place which was used to providing its people with the basics of home, food and work, the denial of such fundamentals was captured most famously by John Steinbeck in his 1939 novel *The Grapes of Wrath*. Indeed, this poignant and epic tale of the migrant Joad family, seeking survival in the "promised land" of California, is believed to have influenced Eleanor Roosevelt in her campaign to improve the lot of migrant workers. John Ford's beautiful film adaptation, a year later, merely added weight to Steinbeck's narrative.

A look at how (and where) the Revolta–Armour final was reported in *The Daily Oklahoman* during these hard times is instructive. Certainly, the sports editor added a dash of color to his story by describing Revolta as a "stout stroker" and reporting of Armour that his "woods sang lustily but whose irons strayed and faltered in the pinches."[67] What was interesting, however, is that this story dominated the front page of a newspaper which had a daily circulation of almost 100,000. Meanwhile, the seemingly far more significant news that Oklahoma was to receive an extra $439,114 in aid from the WPA, presumably to help create more jobs, was relegated to page 2. Such prioritizing of news may have simply been a way of keeping up the reader's spirits during the Depression. Clearly, hosting one of golf's majors was also a source of pride to Oklahomans and therefore a story deserving of its top billing. However, the tournament's

From left to right: **Tommy Armour, Gene Sarazen and Johnny Farrell (courtesy USGA).**

prominence did highlight the fact that despite far more pressing issues, some newspaper editors must have believed that professional golf was capable of maintaining and boosting circulation.

Apart from his billing as a "stout stroker," Revolta believed that his first-round victory over Hagen gave him the confidence to go on and win what proved to be his only major title. However, he was also helped in the final by laying a number of stymies (unintentionally, according to Revolta) against Armour. In those days and until 1951, when it was universally abolished, the stymie was an integral and often controversial part of match-play golf. Based on the "play the ball as it lies" principle, if on the green your ball was impeded by your opponent's ball, and the two balls were within 6 inches of each other, then you had to play it. Opinion was sharply divided on the issue, with some state organizations, such as the Wisconsin Golf Association, abolishing the stymie in local competitions. Unsurprisingly, the view from Scotland, where the stymie originated, was very different. According to *The Glasgow Herald,* "The game would be the poorer for its loss for the successful lofting of a stymie or

Tommy Armour practices his putting (courtesy Tufts Archives, Pinehurst, North Carolina).

the delicate use of borrow with a touch of 'side' is surely among the most satisfying strokes in the whole of golf."[68] Bobby Jones also supported this view. Revolta may have benefited from the stymie in the final, but Armour was in no doubt that it was Johnny's superb short game which made the difference. For his PGA victory, the 24-year-old Revolta received $1,000. In total he won $9,500 in 1935 and finished as the PGA's leading money winner.

As noted elsewhere, one of Bob Harlow's ideas was that the tour should become an "all-year-round affair." While the Depression years did not quite witness this, there is little doubt that the tour did try and spread its wings. For example, after the usual winter/spring tour of 1935, the summer and early autumn months saw a number of events in venues out-

Al Espinosa, one of the many Latin American professionals who made their mark (Photographic History Collection, Division of Information Technology and Communications, National Museum of American History, Smithsonian Institution).

side the usual western and southern states. Hershey, Pennsylvania, for instance, hosted a tournament in both July and August; Chicago, St. Paul, Ohio and Glen Falls, New York, were also among those places that the pros visited. The prize money was modest, with total purses ranging from $1,500 to $5,000, but the tournaments offered the players a chance to make some cash and to keep their games sharp for the PGA title and for the more lucrative winter/spring tour. Financially, it was Harry Cooper who profited most from these events, with victories in St. Paul and Chicago. His total prize money came to $1,950.

One further event of interest in the autumn of 1935 took place at the $5,000 Indianapolis Open, held in October. This saw Al Espinosa achieve the last of his nine tour wins. Espinosa was another of the "golfing brothers" who were so prominent at this time. The Espinosa's rivaled the Turnesa family, as five brothers became professional golfers. Apart from Al, Abe competed on tour and won the Texas Open in 1931, and Ray, Henry and Romie had successful teaching careers. In addition, sister Annette became a teaching pro and for a while in the 1920s, taught at Pebble Beach. Unsurprisingly, in this period she was the only woman golf professional on the West Coast. The Espinosa brothers were yet another example of the professionals with Latin origins who emerged in such numbers at this time. They were also another example of those who graduated from the caddie yard to achieve great prominence in the game of golf. In their case, they caddied and learned the game at the Del Monte course on the Monterey Peninsula.

Al was twice a Ryder Cup player and lost to Bobby Jones in a playoff for the National Open title of 1929 at Winged Foot. This was the championship in which Jones made one of golf's most famous 72nd-hole putts (a downhill, sidehill, 12-footer) to tie Espinosa. The putt, which gave Jones score a 79 after a last-nine collapse, was deemed by O.B. Keeler as the most important of Bobby's career, as he did not believe Jones would have ever recovered from his melt-down. Considering that Jones won the Grand Slam the following year, Keeler's views may have more than a little merit. The previous year, Espinosa was also runner-up in a major—this time to Leo Diegel in the PGA Championship.

What was also notable about the Indianapolis Open was the presence in the field of several members of the British Ryder Cup team, which had just contested the biannual matches at Ridgewood, New Jersey, in late September. This time, the U.S. team won by the comfortable margin of nine points to three, with a formidable list of members which read like a "who's who" of the era. Walter Hagen was captain as usual, and he was joined by Paul Runyan, Sam Parks, Olin Dutra, Ky Laffoon, Johnny Revolta, Henry Picard, Horton Smith, Gene Sarazen and Craig Wood. All of these players, apart from Laffoon, either had won or would win major titles. Apart from the comprehensive victory for the home team, there were two other particular notes of interest. First was the level of interest, with a 10,000-strong crowd following the matches on the first day. Second was the intriguing match between newly crowned U.S. Open champion Sam Parks and Alf Perry, who won the Open Championship at Muirfield that year. One down while playing the 36th hole, Parks continued his wonderful year by holing a 30-foot birdie putt to halve the match.

By the end of 1935, America, under FDR, was making some economic progress, with unemployment dropping from 25 percent to just under 15 percent in many areas. Many of the government-sponsored employment programs were clearly paying off. However, while this progress was welcome, times were still tough, money was scarce, and the Grapefruit Circuit remained a place where only the fittest survived.

CHAPTER 4

The Tour 1936–1940

*"Obscure young Eastern professionals often club together to buy
an old car for the tour of Florida's tournaments, hoping that luck
and the urgent need for a new set of tires will help them win a
slice of the prize money, but they seldom care to risk the trip across
the Rockies where more celebrated practitioners start the money
season"—Time Magazine,* December 31, 1931

This harsh appraisal in *Time Magazine* was a further indication of
the realities of life on tour, at least for some. Certainly the same prize
pattern continued in 1936, with the occasional large winner's check
such as that for the San Francisco Match-play Open won by Willie
Hunter, who received $1,675 for his victory over Willie Goggin.
Hunter was another who had followed the path of many British golfers
in seeking a better life in America. The son of Harry Hunter, who was
the club professional at Deal, the Open Championship venue on the
southeast coast of England, Willie won the 1921 British Amateur at Hoy-
lake in which Bobby Jones competed. In a manner similar to Tommy
Armour, Hunter started his golfing life in America as an amateur; also
like Armour, who became secretary at the Westchester-Biltmore Club,
Willie occupied a similar position at the Rancho Club in Los Angeles.
Here he honed his game by playing with and against California's leading
amateurs, one of whom was George Von Elm, who had moved to the
West Coast a few years earlier. Willie turned pro in 1925 and was
appointed to the Brentwood Club in California. He eventually became
a club professional at the prestigious Riviera Club in Los Angeles, where
he served from 1936 until his retirement in 1964. Notwithstanding
Hunter's large prize in San Francisco, purses were generally modest in

Willie Hunter, one of many British professionals who took up American citizenship and made a better life in their adopted land (courtesy Riviera Country Club).

1936, with, for example, a $3,000 total fund in Sacramento. In this event, Wiffy Cox won first money of $700 and Wild Bill Melhorn got $450 for second place.

Mehlhorn was yet another gift to the golf writers during the 1930s. The name "Wild Bill" came about either because of his temperament or (according to Mehlhorn) because of his ability to shoot really low scores.[1] Regardless of which version is correct, there was no doubting his eccentricities, many of which were in evidence during the 1920s when he was a regular winner and a Ryder Cup player in the inaugural matches of 1927.

About to tee off: from the left, Jimmy Thomson, "the Blonde Bomber" Craig Wood, "Wild" Bill Mehlhorn and Denny Shute (courtesy Tufts Archives, Pinehurst, North Carolina).

For example, it was alleged that on one occasion at the Texas Open, Bobby Cruickshank had two putts to win on the last green when he was distracted by noise from a nearby tree. (In the event Cruickshank four putted.) It was discovered that Mehlhorn was the source of the disturbance and understandably he was accused of bad sportsmanship, even though he was not Cruickshank's nearest rival. The incident became known as "the monkey in the treetop incident." Later in life, Mehlhorn argued that the tree in question was so far away that he could not have upset Cruickshank.[2] A few weeks later the pair met in a play-off for the South Central Open in Arkansas and no hard feelings were in evidence. Mehlhorn won that title, but the "bad boy" label stuck.

On another occasion in Britain, Mehlhorn, as was the norm at a time when professionals were seen as little more than caddies, was refused entry into a clubhouse. Rather than adopt the more gently effective approach of Hagen, who once changed in his chauffeur-driven car outside the clubhouse at Deal, Mehlhorn shoved aside the attendant and barged his way in. Unsurprisingly, the American PGA took a very poor view of his antics.

The early Depression years were not kind to Mehlhorn but having disappeared from view for a while, he reappeared with the backing of the Powerbilt club manufacturer, Hillerich and Bradsby. Mehlhorn was now a somewhat changed man, with his eccentricities being of a more benign nature. For instance, in the 1936 PGA Championship at Pinehurst he used a putter resembling a croquet mallet, which he christened "Annie Oakley" after the famed sharpshooter. He used the putter so effectively that he lost to eventual winner Denny Shute only on the 36th hole of their semi-final match. Despite all of these quirks, Mehlhorn was a thoughtful man when it came to golf technique and wrote the celebrated book *Golf Secrets Exposed*. He was also credited with inventing numbering on golf clubs.

One of the relative newcomers who made an impact in 1936 was Jimmy Hines, a fair-haired former caddie from New York who was playing out of Garden City, Long Island. Hines was another prodigious hitter who the scribes nicknamed "the Blonde Belter" (as opposed to Craig Wood, "the Blonde Bomber"). Hines won three times in 1936, including successive victories on the West Coast. The first of these was at the Riverside Open and the second at the prestigious Los Angeles Open, where the first prize was $1,500. In total Hines won nine tour events during his career and was selected to represent the United States in the 1939 Ryder Cup, which was to be held in America. The matches, however, were canceled due to the outbreak of war in Europe.

Nineteen thirty-six also saw the prodigious Lawson Little turn professional. Little had an unusual introduction to golf. He first started playing the game in China, where his father was stationed as a colonel in the medical corps of the U.S. army. Later the family settled in San Francisco, where Little featured on the Stanford University golf team—a team which later included Tom Watson and Tiger Woods. A burly, broad-shouldered man, his fame owed much to his length but more particularly to his successive wins in both the British and U.S. Amateur Championships in 1934 and 1935. For these achievements Little won the annual Sullivan award, honoring America's outstanding athlete. The only golfer to have previously won this prestigious honor was Jones. When he turned professional in the spring of 1936, Little suggested that he might not play in tour events (apart from the Masters) but instead earn a comfortable living from other golfing sources. This was not quite the "businessman golfer" approach of George Von Elm, in that Von Elm made it clear that he

Lawson Little was one of many athletes to endorse Wheaties, "the Breakfast of Champions" (courtesy General Mills Archives and Lawson Little III).

wanted to compete on tour. But there were some similarities, in that neither man expressed an interest in the life of the club pro.

One of the lucrative avenues open to Little was cashing in on his reputation by endorsing a number of non-golfing products. For example, Little joined the "Wheaties Team," which featured other sporting luminaries such as Lou Gehrig and Babe Ruth from the world of baseball and swimming champion Johnny Weismuller. "Wheaties, the Breakfast of Champions" was the brand's slogan featured regularly in advertisements in the nation's newspapers.

Perhaps the most remarkable of Little's advertisements could be found in a comic strip in the children's section of, among other publications, *The Washington Post*. It highlighted the issue of leading golfers cashing in by endorsing the "twin evils" of tobacco and alcohol. This particular color cartoon charted a path from Little's start in the game, to his amateur successes, to his becoming a professional. According to Little, "I smoke Camels at meals and after ... they bring me a cheery feeling of well-being."[3] This message appeared alongside Dick Tracy, Mickey Finn and The Gumps. The Camel cigarette company was perhaps the firm most associated with professional golf, as Revolta, Shute, Armour, Sarazen and MacFarlane all endorsed the brand. Slogans ranged from "Camels Never Get on Your Nerves" to "For Your Digestion's Sake—Smoke Camels."[4] Denny Shute, in particular, assured the public of the power of Camels when he claimed, "I couldn't have won the British Open if my nerves hadn't been in perfect condition."[5] Johnny Revolta even told the readers that his favorite meal was corned beef and cabbage but that Camels made this taste better.

From the perspective of today, the number of players cashing in on the cigarette business may seem at best surprising and at worst downright exploitative. However, this was long before the "knowledge society"—that is, when the facts associating smoking with poor health became incontrovertible. The 1930s was also a time when smoking was viewed as glamorous, for both men and women. Movie stars, both on and off screen, were regularly seen with a cigarette, as were political figures such as FDR. Paying easily recognizable golf stars to endorse cigarettes was an obvious and understandable marketing strategy of the Depression era. And it was not just tobacco which was endorsed and glamourized by the leading professionals: alcohol was also seen as an off-course source of income.

The idea of contemporary golf stars such as Tiger Woods or Phil Mickleson advertising alcohol is unthinkable, as we live in an era where fitness is an integral part of the professional's life. Daily visits to the gym, nutritionists, and personal trainers are all part of players' lifestyles, as they seek to maximize their potential and gain an advantage over their rivals. A double major winner and 1950s star, Jackie Burke, Jr., liked to joke that in his day, all pros had the same mind guru, Jack Daniels. (A few shots of J.D. after a poor round and your mind was sorted.) However, in the 1930s many leading players found the association with liquor companies more than mentally soothing.

In the first year of FDR's presidency (1933) Roosevelt made good on his election promise to repeal Prohibition. This was a boon to brewers and distillers, who sought to make up for lost time, not to mention the general public, who could legally buy and enjoy liquor. As was often the case during this era, Eleanor Roosevelt captured the right mood. When news broke that light wines would be served at state lunches in Washington, one report read: "Mrs. Roosevelt has shown her characteristic good sense in admitting wine to the White House and is to be congratulated on her patriotic decision to serve only American wines."[6] Golf was also ready to benefit from the repeal of Prohibition, with *Golfdom* magazine predicting that much needed beverage sales at clubs for 1934 would total $15 million, although net profits would be hit owing to the necessity to pay for bar equipment, licenses and insurance.

The repeal of Prohibition was also a bonus for some leading professionals. For example, 1929 U.S. Open Champion, Johnny Farrell claimed, "I can't afford to gamble with my putting touch by drinking inferior whiskies.... I don't drink much whiskey but when I do it's John Jameson." Jameson labeled itself "the Sportsmen's Whiskey" and also used tour regulars Wiffy Cox and Willie MacFarlane to endorse its product. The Farrell advertisement, from *The American Golfer,* also offered a putting tip from the player, no doubt designed to suggest to the reader that Jameson might be an aid to better scores.

Beer also featured, with 1934 U.S. Open champion Olin Dutra being among those who endorsed the Hamm's brand. Similarly, Tommy Armour promoted G&W Gin. Armour was a natural in this regard, as it was no secret that he enjoyed a "nip" from time to time. One of his advertisements for G&W read, "Tommy Armour Makes a Long One at the 19th Hole." This ad featured a recipe for how to make "The Birdie, G&W's June Cooler"—a Martini consisting of a jigger of claret, lime juice, powdered sugar, and a jigger of G&W.

Apart from his relationship with Camel and Wheaties, Lawson Little cashed in on his reputation by signing up to embark on a tour of theaters, where he could demonstrate his talents on stage. He also became part of the "Spalding Fourball" along with Horton Smith, Jimmy Thomson and, eventually, Harry Cooper. This project, aimed at popularizing the game, was directed by Bobby Jones, who expressed his delight "to have Lawson Little with me in this new laboratory experiment for the development of the game."[7]

However, despite his earlier comments, Little soon began competing professionally. To say he was not well received by his fellow professionals would be an understatement. Journalist Henry McLemore wrote that "since he turned pro, Lawson Little has been the most unpopular player among his companions ... they put the chill on him."[8] There were a number of reasons for this. First, his military upbringing was a privileged background far removed from that of the overwhelming number of professionals. Second, when he turned pro, Little did so in a blaze of publicity (and endorsements) following on the heels of his amateur triumphs, which was resented by the touring pros. Third, in a manner akin to the earlier experience of George Von Elm, the professionals resented another amateur joining the paid ranks and taking a slice of the prize money. Fourth, Little's sometimes dour personality did not endear him to the pros or indeed the public. Notwithstanding these problems, Little progressed and in September 1936, he won his first tournament, the Canadian Open, in Ontario. Little went on to win eight tour events. In 1940, he joined a select band who had won both the amateur and professional titles of the United States, when he defeated Gene Sarazen in a play-off at Canterbury.

The 1936 Masters was won by Horton Smith who triumphed at Augusta for a second time. By now "Masters" was gradually replacing the "Augusta National Invitation" name. As with the inaugural event in 1934, the pre-tournament publicity focused on Bobby Jones and how he would perform. Given that he was absent from regular competition for almost six years, and that he experienced something akin to the putting "yips" at the inaugural Masters in 1934, his odds of 6/1 favorite and 8/1 joint favorite with Henry Picard seemed to be based more on sentiment than on reality. In the event, Jones finished 21 shots behind the winning score of 285. Smith owed much of his win to some wonderful putting in the closing stages. Once again, it was Harry Cooper who suffered, as he lost out by a single stroke after a final round of 76. Smith's win was worth $1,500 in prize money.

Denny Shute won the first of two successive PGA titles by defeating Jimmy Thomson 3 and 1 in the final at Pinehurst. Some background to the staging of the championship at Pinehurst provides evidence of, on the one hand, the residual condescension toward professionals that persisted in some quarters and, on the other hand, the prestige which could be gained from hosting one of golf's majors. Earlier we saw how the "gentlemen of the fairways—the fair haired boys" were unreservedly welcomed when the tour stopped at Greensboro. However, the Tufts family, which founded and owned the Pinehurst resort, regularly sponsored the North and South tournament, yet never seemed totally convinced as to the worth of this investment. For example, in 1932, Leonard Tufts argued, "we have thought in the past that the pro at 'Skimville Hollow' who has as his pupils the two nabobs of the town would get said nabobs to pay his expenses and then go home and tell the folks back home how he only missed beating Hagen by fourteen putts."[9] Despite these misgivings about the professional "class," Tufts paid the PGA $12,000 for the privilege of hosting the championship, as he clearly saw one of the four majors as an event which would enhance both Pinehurst's image and tourism revenue.

Indeed, in a letter to a prospective visitor, James Tufts was quick to promote the PGA as part of the resort's plans "for your entertainment." Along with sheltering the clubhouse porch for those who wish to sit in the sun, Tufts called hosting the PGA as being "the most important event taking place in Pinehurst this fall." He went on to say that "we are mighty proud to think that Pinehurst has been so honored."[10] It would seem that Tufts got good value for his money, with the 36-hole decider being something of a contrast in style, as it featured the methodical, 148-pound, understated Shute versus the long-hitting, media-friendly, extremely colorful Thomson.

Denny Shute was the

On the left, Denny Shute, and the "Big Blaster" Jimmy Thomson, before their 1936 PGA Championship final, which Denny won (courtesy Tufts Archives, Pinehurst, North Carolina).

son of an English-born club professional. Herbert Warren Wind described him as being "as loquacious as Calvin Coolidge,"[11] the notoriously silent American president of the 1920s. Certainly Shute was something of an intellectual and for a period attended Western Reserve University, where he was a member of Phi Gamma Delta. He was also a stamp collector. Occasionally, however, Shute gave interviews—and when he did, he was worth listening to. For example, in 1935 he asserted that American courses were too heavily watered and therefore too many players could not play "hard" courses. Typically prefacing his comments with the disclaimer "what I have to say is not of the least importance," he predicted that "the next batch of great golfers will come from the region of Texas and the South, where greater skill in the control of the ball is required. A Texan is at home on any ground and can hold his shot."[12] Considering that in the next 10 years, Nelson, Hogan and Demaret would make their considerable mark on the game, Shute's comments were extremely farsighted.

Shute also had something to say about the cost and exclusive nature of golf in America. Noting that in Dornoch, Scotland, members paid 5 shillings per year dues, largely because the local club was happy to make a very modest annual profit, Shute argued that golf in America should be a "recreation for all classes" and that "golf should be taught in the public schools and by pros who are in sympathy with the instruction of children."[13] Regardless of whether Shute was fully aware of the WPA program for building hundreds of public courses, he was clearly a man who saw the bigger picture as far as golf was concerned.

As a tournament player Shute built up a formidable record during the Depression years. All in all, he won 16 tour events and was a three-time Ryder Cup player, but what separated him from many was his Open Championship success at St. Andrews in 1933, when he beat Craig Wood in a play-off, and the aforementioned successive PGA titles in 1936 and 1937. He also tied for the U.S. Open in 1939 but lost in a play-off to Wood and to the eventual winner, Byron Nelson. Shute may not have received the headlines which came the way of "Slammin" Sam Snead or "Lord" Byron Nelson, but his record as a multiple major winner bears comparison with many of the game's greats.

In contrast to Shute stood Jimmy Thomson, who was born into a thoroughbred golfing family in the Scottish stronghold of North Berwick. His father Wilfred was a professional and his uncle was the legendary Ben Sayers, who twice finished as runner-up in the Open Championship in the days when it was played over 36 holes and who became even more famous as a club designer. The Ben Sayers brand exists to this day. Jimmy's cousin was 1904 Open Championship winner Jack White. When Jimmy was 12, his family emigrated to America. He started playing the game in earnest at the Country Club, West Virginia, where his father was appointed professional.

Thomson developed quickly as a player and finished second to Sam Parks, Jr., in the U.S. Open at Oakmont in 1935. Here he bogeyed the last four holes and surrendered a two-shot lead. Jimmy, however, was not simply a runner-up: he had a number of tournament wins, notably in the Australian Centenary Open of 1934. Here he won in a field which included Sarazen, Shute and Diegel. He also won the Los Angeles Open in 1938.

However, Thomson's fame as a golfer owed more to his driving

The big names of this era needed the financial security of a club job as well as what they could earn on tour, from exhibitions, and from endorsements. Here "the Big Blaster" Jimmy Thomson plays with some club members when he was attached to Broadmoor. Included (second from the right) is Spencer Penrose, who owned the Broadmoor Hotel and Golf Club (courtesy Broadmoor, Colorado Springs).

prowess than anything else. In this regard he was pure "box office"—someone whom sponsors loved to see on the starting list. By the 1930s, steel shafts were being widely used in America[14] and significant manufacturing advances had been made by Wilson and Spalding, to which Jimmy was under contract. Thus Thomson had certain advantages over those who played in the hickory-shafted days. Notwithstanding this, he was unusually long, as evidenced by his reaching the 621-yard 12th hole in two shots during his near miss in Oakmont in 1935. Interestingly, in a 2008 "50 Greatest U.S. Open Moments" article,[15] Britain's *Daily Telegraph* placed at number 23, John Daly's 1993 achievement in reaching Baltusrol's 630-yard 17th hole in two shots—and this was with the benefit of modern golfing technology!

Thomson also gained fame as the husband of former silent screen star, Viola Dana. The couple were married in 1930, in what *The New York Times* described as the movie star's "third venture."[16] Interestingly, it seemed that Viola had a penchant for athletes, as one of her previous husbands was American football star Maurice "Lefty" Flynn. Later in his career, Jimmy would himself dabble in the movie business when appearing in *The Caddy* with Dean Martin and Jerry Lewis.

For the 1936 final, the press accorded Thomson the favorite's tag, which may have been surprising given that Shute was good enough to win the British Open at St. Andrews in 1933 and Thomson had never won a major. As it turned out, it was Shute's straight hitting and steady short game which prevailed. As he wryly commented afterward, "I always consoled myself with the knowledge that while golf has been played many years, they have yet to pay out on the first shot."[17] Shute's prize was $1,000. It is worth noting that in these times, golfers played a 36-hole qualifier before match-play started. Thus, for this prize, apart from qualifying, Shute played three matches over 18 holes and then three more over 36 holes. The $1,000 was hard earned.

A further note of interest in that year's PGA and one which added a dash of color to the event was the presence of Leo "The Walloper" Walper, who took Jug McSpaden to the 19th hole before losing in the third round. Golf fans were told of how Leo was a driving range professional who had been an ambulance driver, a car salesman, an insurance salesman, and a baritone in the church choir. He also decided to try his luck on tour by traveling in a caravan.[18] Indeed at one stage the emerging Sam Snead considered traveling with Walper but in the end decided against it. Thrifty Sam figured that traveling in a car towing a caravan would cost a lot in gas and instead teamed up with Johnny Bulla. Not a

Tony Manero on his way to winning the 1936 U.S. Open at Baltusrol (courtesy Baltusrol Golf Club).

great deal was heard again of "The Walloper" apart from the occasional sub-par round and a 30-day suspension for an "ethics" violation in 1938. (Walper claimed this was just personal business between himself and George Jacobus.)

The National Open was won that year by Tony Manero, who somewhat unexpectedly won at Baltusrol from Harry Cooper. Manero's victory may have been something of a surprise, but not on the same scale as that of Sam Parks the previous year. Often referred to in the newspapers as "the dapper little Italian," Manero was one of the increasing band of American golfers who grew up and caddied in the Westchester area of New York County. Indeed, in the Fairview Country club where Manero learned his trade, other caddies included four members of the Turnesa family; a U.S. Open champion, Johnny Farrell; and Willie Creavy, brother of former PGA champion Tom.

Manero's win was deemed controversial as some believed that his final round partner, his fellow Italian American Gene Sarazen, helped him over the finishing line. In the end, the USGA deemed that Sarazen had offered encouragement rather than advice to the new champion. Based on Manero's "How to Win the Open" article published after the event, it would appear the correct decision was made. For example, after going out in 33 in the final round, Sarazen said to him, "You're burning up the course Tony. This is your day if you keep up the pace." And when, deep into the back nine, a spectator asked Manero, "How can I cure an awful slice," Manero showed commendable restraint and it was Gene who led the fan away.[19] Such examples would seem to come under the heading of encouragement and sportsmanship rather than anything untoward.

Manero would become a Ryder Cup player the following year and in total he won eight official titles on tour. Interestingly, his predecessor as National Open champion, Sam Parks, gave Manero a piece of succinct advice on how best to take advantage of his newfound fame: "Get the dough in the first month or you'll never get it."[20] Parks's view was based on personal experience, as he claimed he made $17,000 from his 1935 National Open victory, mostly by way of exhibition matches. One of these was a match with legendary British golfer Joyce Wethered, who was touring America at the time. With no women's professional tour in those days, Ms. Wethered cashed in on her outstanding ability and reputation by endorsing equipment and by playing exhibitions. Billed as "the Queen of Golf," her 10-week American tour was sponsored by the same Wanamaker family which had been so instrumental in establishing the PGA. Seeing the potential for growth in women's golf, the Wanamaker store chain arranged the tour to help promote Joyce Wethered golf equipment. Her trip included matches with or against Bobby Jones, Leo Diegel and her old amateur adversary, Glenna Collet Vare. On the occasion of her match against the U.S. Open champion, when Parks heard that Wethered was being paid $350, he asked for and received the same amount. This,

Tony Manero and his playing partner for the final round at Baltusrol, Gene Sarazen. The pairing led to a brief USGA inquiry, as it was suggested that Sarazen had "helped" his fellow Italian American. The inquiry found no wrongdoing (courtesy Baltusrol Golf Club).

Parks recalled, was well above the normal $150.[21] Sam won the contest with a 73 to Joyce's 80.

Manero paid attention to Parks's suggestion by embarking on a quick exhibition tour to South America with Johnny Revolta. This netted him $2,000. Then in April 1937, he became head pro at the Salem Country Club, Massachusetts. As we know, it was not unusual for a professional, after winning a major or a series of important events, to capitalize on his success by acquiring a more lucrative contract for representing another club. Henry Picard and his association with Hershey was a prime example. And like Picard, who was supported by Milton Hershey, the candy bar tycoon, Manero benefited from kindly and wealthy club benefactors. In this case it was Ed Winslow and Ed Poor of the host club who guaranteed Manero's contract in Salem. The club committee had stipulated an annual contract of not more than $1,000 for a new professional, but it was widely known among the members that Manero earned considerably more than this.[22] One further note of interest from 1936 was that Ralph Guldahl continued his comeback by winning the Radix Cup for the year's best scoring average with 71.63.

Also of importance in 1936 was the ongoing evolution of Bob Harlow's expansionist plans in July and August, when the tour moved to the Pacific Northwest. The trip to the Northwest was in a sense a mini-tour as it comprised a four-week loop at a cost of approximately $400 per person. Local newspapers referred to this "swing" as "the Evergreen Trail" and were delighted that "big leaguers" such as Sarazen, Runyan, Guldahl, and Tony Manero, made the trip. In particular, Seattle journalist Virginia Boren warmed to the story and predicted that the local tournament would not only be a "magnet for the contestants but golf fans will come from all parts of the country and will give Seattle a very gay and busy summer season socially. Many luncheons, dinners and dances will be arranged."[23] Ms. Boren's comments may seem a little extravagant, but regardless of the tournament's "social" success, it was estimated that over 6,000 people attended the tournament. Admission was $1.10, including tax.

Incidentally, the $400 expenses included a trip by train and boat to and from Chicago, along with the usual outgoings of caddie fees, food and rooms, which were $2.50 per day. Notwithstanding what seemed like good value for the professionals, Byron Nelson's wife, Louise, did not make the trip as the couple could not afford the extra travel fare.[24] Harlow witnessed the trip at first hand and as ever was quick to point out its advantages to sponsors and players alike: "Players who made this tour will never forget it and will repeat it often. It compares with the winter tour, when the boys go south to keep warm. In summer, go to the Pacific Northwest and keep cool."[25]

Where the golf was concerned, it was an excellent trip for the emerging Byron Nelson, who won a total of $2,151 from the four stops. All of this was accomplished without winning a tournament. The honors went to veteran MacDonald Smith at Seattle, who beat Ralph Guldahl in a play-off, 65–71. For this, Smith received the very healthy sum of $1,700, with Guldahl taking home $750.

Horton Smith won at Victoria and Ray Mangrum was victorious at Portland. The name Mangrum usually conjures up images of Lloyd, who would become a U.S. Open winner and Ryder Cup captain in the future. However, as the older brother, Ray was the first to make his name in golf. Another of the emerging Texas professionals of which Denny Shute spoke, Ray had a successful playing career with many fine finishes and five tournament victories. In the 1940s, he also contributed in a small but significant way to golfing history when he mentored one of the first African American professionals to come to national prominence, Ted Rhodes. In fact, Rhodes was sent to Ray by heavyweight champion Joe Louis, who was a serious golfer and who had employed Ted as his personal teacher. At this time, membership in the PGA still contained a "Caucasians only" clause, but now and again some more liberal sponsors invited black professionals to play in their tournaments. The Tam O Shanter, for instance, invited Rhodes and other black players to compete. However, the 1948 Los Angeles Open was the first official PGA event to open its doors to African Americans; two black pros Ted Rhodes and Bill Spiller, competed, with Ted finishing in the money in a respectable 21st place. After winning his first Masters in 1997, Tiger Woods paid tribute to three "minority" golfers who had blazed a trail for him: Lee Elder, Charlie Sifford and Ted Rhodes.

The remaining event on the Evergreen Trail, at Vancouver, was won by the amateur Ken Black, who shot a last round of 63 on this, his home course. Nelson and Thomson finished second, so they took home a split of the first and second cash prizes—$975. It was not unusual for amateurs to tee it up with the professionals during this era and a number of "State Opens" were sanctioned by the PGA as official events. After all, a tournament was a tournament. Apart from Ken Black, several other amateurs won official tour events, including Jim Milward, who won the Wisconsin title in 1937 and 1938.

As far as the Evergreen Trail went, with over $2,000 in prize money and expenses of roughly $400, it is clear that these were profitable weeks for Nelson. Similarly, eight other leading players, including Guldahl, Thomson and Smith, all won in excess of $1,000 during the trip. However, Harlow reported that the sponsors at Vancouver, Victoria and Seattle all incurred losses but "were well satisfied with the ventures and seek dates on a permanent tour."[26]

Overall, the new venture was deemed a success and a further indication that the game and its leading players were moving forward. However, the fact that the tour was still a work in progress was confirmed by the comments of the vastly experienced PGA committee chairman Horton Smith, who, as well as competing, monitored the players' performances and behavior. After the Pacific Northwest tour, Smith declared that "the golf has been up to the high standard which has been obtained by

Sam Snead in familiar pose (courtesy Tufts Archives, Pinehurst, North Carolina).

the American professional ... as a whole the boys conducted themselves well and made a good impression." However, he went on, "a few boys have not learned that they must not use the fairways of host clubs for practice."[27] Perhaps in defense of the players, practice facilities were not what they later became. However, it was a sign of the PGA's growing professionalism that it was conscious of the need for the still fledgling tour to achieve and maintain certain standards.

Unfortunately for Harlow (and maybe for the Pacific Northwest), his days as tournament director were coming to a close and the immediate years ahead did not see a repeat of this mini-tour. However, in time Seattle and Portland regularly hosted tournaments, and in so doing vindicated the PGA's tournament director's foresight.

Nineteen thirty-seven was the year in which Sam Snead announced his arrival on tour. A practice of this era was for top equipment manufacturers to use their established contracted stars to look out for promising newcomers. In the case of Dunlop, Craig Wood was one of its name players; he helped Snead gain a contract with Dunlop worth a signing-on fee of $500. Being raw and inexperienced in such matters, Sam was somewhat confused when Henry Picard took him aside before the 1936 Hershey Open. "In the tourney," Picard said, "you'll be paired with Craig Wood. I'll give you a tip. Wood represents the Dunlop Tire & Rubber, one of the big golf-ball makers. I think he's considering you for Dunlop."

"Considering me for what?" Snead replied.

"I mean he may sign you up as a Dunlop representative."

To which Snead replied, "My God."[28]

With his long driving, Snead impressed the "Blonde Bomber" enough to be offered a contract, and the money helped launch Sam's career. The deal included two dozen balls per month plus a set of Dunlop clubs. However, the following year Snead signed with Wilson and began an association with that company which lasted for the remainder of his life. In total Snead won five times in 1937. One of these victories came at the inaugural Bing Crosby Pro-Am, then held at the Rancho Santa Fe club in California. (It later moved north to Pebble Beach.) When recalling the first holding of the Crosby 40 years later, Fred Corcoran made it easy to understand why the stop became so popular with the pros.

As we have seen, in these tough times the tour was not always glamorous. Certainly there was plenty of publicity for the tournament winners and the stop at Pinehurst, with its beauty parlors, was popular with those wives who could afford to travel with their husbands. But day-to-day life was basic, to say the least, with modest accommodations and dining rooms being the norm rather than the exception. However, at the 1937 Crosby, there was a break from the weekly grind. As Corcoran recalled, because of rain, play was washed out on the Saturday and many pros headed for the next tournament thinking there would be no play over the weekend. Those who stayed over included Harry Cooper, Denny Shute, Johnny Revolta and Sam Snead, and all were guests that night at a party hosted by Bing Crosby. As Corcoran described it, "the place was crawling with

Jules Huot, the first Canadian to win on the U.S. tour (courtesy Golf Canada).

movie stars," some of whom included Rita Hayworth and Humphrey Bogart.[29] Fred also recalled that the local "It Café" was very popular with the pros. Fittingly, the café belonged to the original "It Girl," former silent screen star Clara Bow. From that week on, "The Crosby" became known among the professionals as a tour stop that promised fun as well as the chance of a decent payday. Snead was particularly lucky that he decided to stay over, as play was possible on Sunday and he won both the professional and pro-amateur events. In typical fashion, he asked Bing if he might have his $762.50 winnings in cash rather than a check. Even at this early stage of his career, the careful hillbilly image, nurtured by Fred Corcoran, was gaining pace.

Overall, in 1937, with Corcoran's promptings there was more money on offer but purses in many cases remained weighted in favor of the leaders. It was very much a case of only the fittest surviving, with prizes usually provided only to those finishing in the top 15 or 20 places. In the Oakland California Open, for instance, Snead won first prize of $1,200, but only the top 15 finishers received money. There was $80 for 15th place, but the remaining 37 pros went away empty handed. Similarly, at the prestigious Los Angeles Open, from a total purse of $8,000, Harry Cooper won the sizeable first prize of $2,500, with Guldahl and Horton Smith picking up $1,250 each for finishing tied for second. By now Bob Harlow was writing a column for Florida's *Evening Independent* and in his report on the Los Angeles. Open, he commented that "all but the crumbs of the eight grand" went to the first eight.[30] As someone who had campaigned vigorously for a better deal for the professionals, Harlow was better placed than most to comment on the situation. However, he also recorded that the tournament committee added approximately 20 prizes of $25 each, but only after the pros had registered a complaint. Among those receiving the $25 were big names such as Paul Runyan and Craig Wood. The days of the safety net were still a long way away.

The year 1937 also saw the professionals make one of their rare trips across the Canadian border to Ontario for the third and final staging of the General Brock Open—again at the Lookout Point club. This event was interesting for a number of reasons. First, the winner was the French Canadian professional Jules Huot; in doing so, he became the first Canadian to win on tour. No Canadian would repeat this feat until Al Balding won the Mayfair Open in 1957. Second, a young Ben Hogan won some much-needed cash in a long driving contest by placing second to the renowned big hitter Jimmy Thomson. Thomson's longest blow was a staggering 386 yards, while Hogan's drives averaged 330 yards. Third, Walter

"Lord" Byron Nelson in action at the 1935 North and South in Pinehurst (courtesy Tufts Archives, Pinehurst, North Carolina).

Hagen, present no doubt to boost the attendance numbers, suggested that the Lookout Point course was more suited to mountain goats than golfers.[31] Clearly, Sir Walter's status placed him above the earlier PGA directive that players should not criticize the host club.

December 1937 witnessed one of the decade's most colorful players win the Hollywood Beach Hotel Open and a first prize of $750. This was Leonard Dodson, one of the game's great hustlers. Sam Snead, who never played without a bet on the outcome, declared that "with that big black cigar in his mouth, Dodson was about the meanest operator I ever saw when the chips were on the table. While he never won any major world title, a bet made him all but unbeatable."[32] The importance of betting in this harsh era should not be underestimated: apart from prize money and whatever could be made from club duties, the other source of revenue for golfers was gambling. In this regard, Dodson came up with a variety of ways to entice his "pigeons" and he would back himself to beat local amateurs playing on one foot, blindfold, or playing with a tennis ball. Dodson served his gambling apprenticeship at the feet of Titanic Thompson, the legendary hustler who would bet on golf (he could play either right- or left-handed), cards, or anything else. The name "Titanic" came about because he could "sink anything." Thompson was reputed to have killed five men; all, it seems, were either cases of "justifiable homicide" or self-defense. Dodson learned well under Thompson, and it was claimed that before he turned professional, Dodson toured the country and earned the name "thousand dollars Dodson." This was a reference to the sizeable sums he won for his backers. At Hollywood Beach he beat Horton Smith in a play-off, which was a gift for the golf journalists: both men came from Springfield and caddied together as kids, and it was Smith who got Dodson his first club job in Wisconsin. Later, in 1941, Dodson won the team event at the Crosby tournament in the company of Ray Watson, father of eight-time major winner Tom.

Nineteen thirty-seven was a wonderful year for Byron Nelson, who won the sizeable $3,000 first prize by defeating Henry Picard in the final of the Belmont Match-Play Open. The total purse here was $12,000 and Picard received $2,000 as runner-up. However, it was his victory in the Masters which really heralded the start of Lord Byron's great years. He was not considered a favorite before the event; indeed, when he won, one headline read, "Outsider Wins in Augusta Play."[33] The tournament was decided on the back nine and in particular on the 12th and 13th holes. Long before Herbert Warren Wind came up with the name "Amen Corner" to describe the 11th, 12th and 13th holes, this stretch was capable of providing plenty of drama. In this case, Nelson trailed Ralph Guldahl by four when he stood on the 12th tee. Fortunately for Byron, he was playing directly behind Guldahl and witnessed him taking a penalty drop from Rae's Creek. Later he recalled that "watching his misfortunes, I suddenly felt like a light bulb went off in my head."[34] Byron went on a birdie/eagle run of 2/3 against Guldahl's 5/6, and thereby gained a two-shot lead which he maintained to the end. Nelson's winning score was 283 and his prize was $1,500.

Notwithstanding the financial rewards from 1937, like many more pros at this time, Byron felt he also needed the security of a club job. Early in 1937, Byron left Ridgewood and George Jacobus to become head pro at Reading. (Jacobus recommended him for the post.) Later that year, Nelson's salary at Reading rose from $3,750 to a "guaranteed" $5,000 per year. However, what this meant was that if Byron did not make $5,000 from teaching and his shop, the club made up the difference. However, two years later he was appointed head professional at the prestigious Inverness Club in Toledo, Ohio, where his salary would be $3,600 per year and he got to keep all the profits from his club activities, including the shop. By then, Nelson was National Open champion and had a new MacGregor equipment contract. Despite this, Nelson believed that "he needed that club job to survive."[35] And in an ironic microcosm of his (then) supremacy over his friend and rival Ben Hogan, it was Hogan who was the second choice of the Inverness Club board.

Nelson's defeated opponent at Augusta in 1937, Ralph Guldahl, had his triumph a few weeks later, when he won the first of his two successive National Open titles. The golf writers did not come up with a nickname for Ralph, although some fans called him the "Depression Champ."[36] This description, it appears, owed more to his aloof demeanor, rather than his being an inspiration for the people in these difficult times. Guldahl was a tall, self-taught Texan. While many of the decade's leading professionals such as Sarazen and Revolta came from Italian stock, Guldahl was the first from Norwegian origins to break through as a professional golfer. *Time Magazine*, as always, had a colorful take on this turn of events: "Invented by Scotch shepherds, golf in the U.S. has been inherited by many Italian day laborer's sons, who caddied on the courses their fathers tended. Guldahl is the first ex-caddie of Norwegian descent to develop top-flight golfing talent."[37] Leaving aside the questionable claim as to the role Scottish shepherds played in the "Royal and Ancient" game, this brief social history of the game's participants was further evidence of the ongoing, immigrant-driven, "melting pot" concept in American golf.

In 1931 at age 19, Guldahl had become one of the youngest winners ever on tour. At this stage his talent was not in doubt and he was regarded as a far superior player to his traveling companion to local tournaments in Texas, Ben Hogan. Another companion from those days was Jack Grout, who was assistant professional at the Glen Garden club where both Hogan and Nelson were introduced the game. Grout competed on tour for many years with just limited success, but he became internationally well known as the one and only teacher of Jack Nicklaus.

Despite the promising start to his professional career, in 1935 Guldahl appeared to lose confidence in his game and was finding it impossible to make a living on tour. The extent to which he was struggling was captured in the *Evening Independent* by Bob Harlow, not long after he left his job as tournament director. Harlow wrote that Guldahl had been

Ralph Guldahl in full flow (courtesy USGA).

A bronze statue of Ralph Guldahl at the Braemar Club, California, where he served as professional and director of golf between 1959 and 1987. It is a fitting tribute to a wonderful player (courtesy Braemar Country Club).

helped by some of his fellow professionals when he was at a low ebb and that he had personally seen the future major winner and three other pros in a "broken-down flivver" traveling from Miami to California to make the next tournament. According to Harlow, the wives had to stay in Florida to save on expenses.[38] Similarly, Paul Mickelson, under a headline of "Guldahl Turns Back Life as an Auto Salesman to Become Leading Golfer,"[39] brought the readers the real life story of how Ralph had left the tour a few years earlier, broke and disenchanted, and went as far as filing an application for a job as a car salesman.

However, with some financial backing and encouragement from Wilson Sporting Goods, Guldahl decided to try again. His return proved to be a great decision, as he dominated the game in the latter stages of the decade. Apart from winning successive U.S. Opens in 1937 and 1938 and the Masters in 1939, Guldahl also won the Western Open in 1936, 1937 and 1938. In those days, the Western Open mirrored today's Players Championship, in that many believed it was in effect the "fifth major." It certainly was a prestigious event. Guldahl's tournament victories totaled 16, and he also played in the Ryder Cup of 1937.

Perceptions of Guldahl's seemingly aloof and at times difficult behavior had some basis in fact. In one report, the outspoken and politically minded Henry McLemore picked up a story on how the Italian Fascist government of Mussolini had introduced a law which allowed police to arrest sportsmen who were guilty of improper language or of throwing objects. McLemore surmised that if such laws were introduced in the United States, the golfing "Sing Sing" team would include Lawson Little, Ralph Guldahl and Harry Cooper, all of whom liked to throw things.[40]

The mention of Guldahl in this piece was not random but was based on personal experience. In another report, McLemore had no hesitation in taking the reigning National Open champion to task for his temper. This was in relation to a PGA championship match between Guldahl and Dick Metz, in which Guldahl flung his club to the ground after Metz laid him a stymie. This, according to McLemore, turned the gallery against Guldahl. In fact, McLemore went on to compare Guldahl to boxer Jack Sharkey, whose seeming arrogance led to "the customers exulting in his troubles."[41] However, there is also evidence that at times Guldahl was agreeable when it came to his dealings with the press. The more recent and wonderful golf writer Dan Jenkins likes to refer to himself as a "quote guy," and it seems that golf writers from the 1930s were well versed in the art of offering the reader words direct from the leading players. Usually these informal interviews took place at the back of the 18th green on the completion of a round. Gene Sarazen was particularly accommodating to journalists eager for some copy. However, Paul Mickleson of the Associated Press, in his syndicated coverage of Guldahl's win at Oakland Hills, claimed to have had a conversation with the winner on the 10th tee of his final round. According to Mickleson, Guldahl told him, "If I can't break 39 on this last nine, just write a story about me saying I'm a bum."[42] Breaking 39 was no easy task on the tough Oakland Hills course, as a vivid report by Charles Bartlett confirms.

A Chicago native, Bartlett began his involvement in sports by selling hot dogs at White Sox baseball games.[43] He became golfing editor of *The Chicago Tribune* in 1931. His interest in golf in his native city, however, went well beyond his reporting duties, as evidenced by his co-founding the *Chicago Tribune* Golf School. This initiative involved 27 local courses making their facilities available to provide free golf instruction for people of all ages. Approximately 15,000 individuals attended the opening day on May 22, 1933, and the Golf School became the model for other similar programs throughout the land.

With William D. Richardson, Bartlett was also involved in founding the Golf Writers' Association and he, too, had an award named after him. This award was established in 1970, three years after Bartlett's death, and is given to those in the game who are considered to have made an outstanding charitable contribution to society. The recipients include Tiger Woods, Payne Stewart and Billy Casper.

In Bartlett's 1937 report, the reader is a given a strong sense of the strain Guldahl played under—"pressure such as few have endured."[44] This was long before the days when the leaders went out last. Guldahl was still

"Lighthorse" Harry Cooper was a prolific winner during the Depression era. Here he receives the winner's check for the 1937 Los Angeles Open (courtesy USGA).

playing the eighth hole when Sam Snead finished with 283—a score many, notably the galleries, thought would be good enough to win. Bartlett painted a picture of this scene for his readers as follows: "But the scrambled platoons of human beings who ran and puffed over the Oakland Hills fairways were unaware of what Guldahl was doing and he made the turn in 33, three under par. They had remained faithful in the fashion of golf galleries to the front runner who in this case was Snead. The young man, by the way, lived up to the prophets' promises for few twenty-four-year-olds playing in their first open come as close as Master Snead did today."[45]

These few lines paid considerable respect to the wonderful challenge of Snead but also set the scene for Bartlett's description of how Guldahl played the back nine. "Adversity Finds a Conquer"[46] was Bartlett's way of summing up how the new champion met all the challenges of the treacherous closing holes. "His drive at the 10th turned up in the wiry grass for which Oakland Hills is famed. His second was in the same tangled grass and after one more swipe at the ball, still remained there. One of those sevens or eights which smash championship hopes was imminent. Guldahl met the emergency by pitching up within two feet of the hole and dropping the putt for a five."[47] Guldahl eventually came home in 36 shots to win by two and definitively prove he was not a "bum."

What was also noteworthy about the National Open was the large crowds who attended Oakland Hills. As we have seen earlier, golf became an outlet for many during this trend decade, and the large crowds who came to watch the professionals bears testimony to this. With affordable admission prices (usually $1), tournaments and exhibitions drew large crowds. For Guldahl's victory, William D. Richardson recorded that a gallery of 10,000 people were "milling around him as he and Harry Cooper started their final journey around the sun-drenched Oakland Hills course."[48] And it was not just the majors which drew large crowds. As noted earlier, 6,000 attended the 1936 Seattle Open. At the same year's Canadian Open, won by Lawson Little, the final-day reports record that "a gallery of 10,000 behaved like a baseball crowd cheering and whistling after every good shot."[49]

This was also the year of Harry Cooper. "Lighthorse Harry" may be best remembered as the man who nearly won a major title, notably in 1936 when Horton Smith beat him by one in the Masters. Similarly, in the 1936 U.S. Open at Baltusrol, Cooper posted the excellent score of 284, despite a weak finish, but lost out to the lesser-known Tony Manero, who beat him with a score of 282. Notwithstanding these disappoint-

ments, Cooper was an excellent player who won 31 professional tournaments during his career, many during the Depression years. The English-
born Cooper was also regarded as a supreme shot-maker, notably with
the wooden clubs, and in 1937 he was the first winner of the Vardon Trophy for the lowest scoring average on the tour. Cooper was also seen both
by journalists and his peers as somewhat eccentric. Before the 14-club
rule was introduced, he regularly carried up to 25 clubs in his bag.

The "Lighthorse" tag came from the celebrated writer Damon Runyon, who regularly covered golf as a Universal Service Staff correspondent
during the 1920s. His columns were widely syndicated. When Cooper
won the first Los Angeles Open in 1926, Runyon wrote: "Mr. Lighthorse
Harry Cooper always moves so fast that he gives the impression of running anyway and with the pack behind him on the jump it only needed
some one to raise a cry of 'Stop thief.'[50]

Cooper was also something of a free spirit in other ways, as evidenced by his "on-off" approach to the security of a club job, which was
sought by most players. He was appointed head professional at the Glen
Oak Country Club, Chicago, in 1930. As the son of an English-born professional who was once apprenticed to Old Tom Morris at St. Andrews,
Cooper certainly had club golf in his veins. Glen Oak was delighted to
have such a prestigious name as head pro and gave him ample time to
play the emerging tour. In return, Harry taught the members for $1.50
per half hour and enhanced the prestige of Glen Oak by arranging for
some of his illustrious peers to play exhibition matches at the club. One
of these took place in July 1932, when Cooper teamed up with Horton
Smith to play Tommy Armour and Gene Sarazen in an 18-hole match.
Once again, the way in which professional golf captured the imagination
of the public was in evidence, as over 5,000 people came to see the stars
and the admission price for a family of six, for example, was $5.[51]

In 1937, however, Cooper made the same journey as Smith and began
working for Spalding along with playing the tour. This was Cooper's best
competitive year and as well as winning his prize money, he also benefited
from his employer's bonus system. For example, in this stellar year Cooper
won seven individual events as well as two fourballs with Horton Smith.
For these successes, "Lighthorse" received bonuses totaling $10,000.[52]
This figure suggests that Cooper received almost $1,000 per win, or the
equivalent of a significant first-prize check. All of this, in addition to his
$14,000 tournament earnings for the year, amounted to considerable
money during the Depression era.

In 1937, Cooper was the first recipient of the Vardon Trophy for the best scoring average. In fact, the tour had offered a consistency award since 1934, which was donated by and named after Harry Radix, president of the Chicago Golf Association. The new award, with its illustrious name, went on to become one of the game's most coveted prizes, bearing names such as Snead, Nicklaus and Woods.

The Ryder Cup of 1937 was held in England, again in Southport. The American team was led by Hagen for the sixth and final time, but one name missing from the American line-up was the leading money winner, Harry Cooper. Along with Jimmy Thomson, Harry did not qualify because he was born in Britain. This "rule" was regularly criticized by players and media alike. The U.S. team created a little piece of history as their victory by seven points to three was the first by an "away" team in the series. This was also the occasion in which Sam Snead began his illustrious Ryder Cup career. The match included a little controversy as, in a precursor of more recent times, complaints were made regarding bad sportsmanship by the galleries. Most notable of these was a suggestion by Ed Dudley that his singles opponent, Alf Perry, had his ball moved closer to the hole by an overly enthusiastic gallery. The most vociferous complainant, however, was Ralph Guldahl, who felt the crowds had been overly partisan in favor of the home team, despite his gaining a comfortable singles victory over Alf Padgham. Needless to say, the British team rejected these allegations, with Arthur Lacey suggesting that "perhaps it would be a good thing if he [Guldahl] doesn't come back. I thought he was a rather difficult fellow, especially when things were going against him." Nor did Guldahl receive a great deal of support from his own side, with the always diplomatic Byron Nelson (who had lost to Dai Rees) asserting, "Why wouldn't 20,000 British fans crowding the courses where we played cheer their home players and pull against us."[53] When Guldahl returned home, PGA President George Jacobus asked him to issue an apology. Ralph expressed some regret but stressed that his comments had been misinterpreted.

As was seen in 1933, U.S. Ryder Cup teams usually competed in the British Open during the "away" years. By this, the third decade of the century, there was little doubting America's global golfing supremacy—and winning the British title was a way of reminding everyone of that fact. Jones in 1930, Armour (a nationalized American) in 1931 and Sarazen in 1932 had all proved the point. In 1933 at St. Andrews, when the U.S. Ryder Cup team had last competed, Shute beat Craig Wood in a play-off. Even if the three previous British Opens had been won by home players, surely this outcome could be attributed to the fact that

only a few Americans competed. That American players did not enter in these years was often a source of criticism both at home and abroad. Certainly there were exceptions, such as Sarazen, who usually played, but the cost of making the trip was high and was seen as the main reason why American professionals stayed at home. This may seem like a weak excuse when set against the chance of putting your name on the claret jug alongside Vardon, Jones and Hagen, but Byron Nelson reckoned his 1937 trip for the Ryder Cup and British Open championship cost him $700 to $800 out of pocket—and this after finishing fifth in the Open. The boat ticket alone cost $1,020 and in these difficult times the PGA covered only some of the Ryder Cup players' expenses.[54]

A further expense was the cost of wives traveling to Britain. Notwithstanding this, some wives (and one in particular) were determined to make the trip, and not just to cheer on their husbands. In this regard, Ralph Guldahl's wife, Laverne, gave an insight into one of the perils of being married to a famous golfer. Ralph and his future wife met when Laverne signed up for six golf lessons. Soon after, they ran away and got married. When accompanying Ralph to the Ryder Cup matches, Laverne told a local reporter that "any woman married to a golf champion would be a fool to let him out of her sight for long. I don't mean that you can't trust the men—it's the girl golf fans you can't trust. There's something about a golfing champion which seems to fascinate the average woman."[55] Laverne's answer, it seems, was because "my Ralph is particularly handsome"—she would not "take any chances" and would stay close to her husband as much as possible.[56]

Thus the U.S. team of 1937 which won the Ryder Cup would have been expected to provide the winner of golf's oldest major championship. After all, a line-up which included proven major winners such as Sarazen, Guldahl and Smith, along with two formidable rookies in the shape of Snead and Nelson, would surely deliver the trophy. The British press appeared to share this view and wondered if any home player could stop "America" from winning. In the end, the U.S. team's combined talent could not prevent Henry Cotton from winning his second British Open title at Carnoustie. Nelson's fifth place was the best the U.S. players could

Opposite: **The 1937 U.S. Ryder Cup side, which became the first "away" team to win the trophy. Note the official outfits complete with the American crest. From left to right, back row: Walter Hagen (captain), Ed Dudley, Henry Picard, Gene Sarazen, Sam Snead, Horton Smith, and Fred Corcoran (manager). From left to right, front row: Byron Nelson, Tony Manero, Ralph Guldahl, Denny Shute, and Johnny Revolta (courtesy Judy Corcoran).**

muster. Long after the dust had settled, the nationalistic element endured when in its golfing review of the year, *The Glasgow Herald* proclaimed that "American dominance had been ended, Cotton had won and what is almost as important, his nearest challengers in the end were British professionals."[57]

Shortly after the British Open had finished, the third chapter in the 1937 saga of America versus Britain took place. This came in the form of a "World Golf Championship," not unlike Henry Doherty's brainchild a few years earlier, but this time arranged by the British *News of the World* newspaper. The format would pit the top British player against his American counterpart. The British choice was easy—Cotton—but the United States had two options: National Open winner Ralph Guldahl or PGA winner Denny Shute, who had successfully defended his title that year with a win over Jug McSpaden. The final, played in front of 5,000 people, was a tense affair which Shute eventually won on the 37th hole. Furthermore, on his way to the final, Shute had beaten Joe Turnesa, Olin Dutra, Jimmy Hines and Tony Manero. As it turned out, PGA President George Jacobus decided that as the challenge was over 72 holes of match-play, it should be Shute. The match took place at the Walton Heath club near London.

Perhaps because the full might of America's professionals could not take the Open trophy back across the Atlantic, the American media were not greatly impressed by Cotton's personality, believing it to be dour in the extreme. One newspaper described him as an "unsociable cuss."[58] "Henry Cotton glowering like the villain in a heavy melodrama"[59] was how another newspaper portrayed him. This was interesting, as his opponent, the cerebral Shute, was certainly not known for his loquaciousness or sparkling personality.

Cotton was also deemed to be something of a snob who "doffs his topper [and] adjusts the knot of his old school tie and in the clipper voice of Mayfair says exactly nothing."[60] The description of Cotton's elitist bearing and background may have been something of an exaggeration, although he did enjoy a far more privileged upbringing than most of his contemporaries. Nevertheless, when he turned professional, his advantaged background did not help him avoid the basic requirements of starting life in his chosen profession. In this regard, he served his time as assistant at the Fulwell club; as the junior in the shop, he learned, among other basic duties, how to sandpaper club heads. Furthermore, whatever was said about his image, perceived or otherwise, one quality Cotton did not lack was dedication to becoming a champion golfer. Long before intense practicing became the norm for professionals, his commitment in this area was well known.

Cotton was also criticized for arriving at tournaments in a chauffeured Rolls Royce, whereas Hagen (who was a big influence on the young Cotton) was praised for doing just the same. The newspapers did conclude, however, that he was probably the best player in the world at that time[61] and his 6/5 win over Shute gave him that status, at least unofficially. For his win Cotton received the equivalent of $2,500 while Shute got just $500. This reward, with the financial contribution the Ryder Cup players received from the PGA, may have just about helped him cover his expenses for his British trip.

The year 1938 began with the USGA introducing the 14-club rule, which has endured to this day. Before this, players could, and often did, carry between 20 and 30 clubs. For example, Wild Bill Mehlhorn regularly carried five woods and 16 irons; Johnny Revolta, five woods and 15 irons; and Harry Cooper, six woods and 16 irons. (The eccentric Leo Diegel reputedly used to carry 36 clubs, which made him very unpopular with the caddies.) Initially, what some players did was take more than the permitted 14 clubs out for practice rounds and then decide which were most suited when the event started. January 1938 also saw Babe Zaharias become the first woman on record to play in a men's PGA tournament, when she teed it up at the Los Angeles Open. This was roughly a decade before Patty Berg, Louise Suggs and others (backed by Fred Corcoran) started the LPGA tour, so a woman playing in a professional tournament was something of a novelty. Unfortunately, the Babe missed the cut with rounds of 84 and 81.

In 1938 the sponsor of previous years, the local chamber of commerce, could not come up with the prize fund, so *The Los Angeles Times* stepped in to the tune of $8,000. One of the advantages of this relationship was that the newspaper could generate a great deal of publicity both for its own tournament and for the professional game. In this regard it was fortunate that Grantland Rice, who tended to winter on the West Coast and who was a member of Lakeside where the Los Angeles Open was often held, was on hand to report on the tournament. In this instance and in reference to Jimmy Thomson's win, Rice enjoyed a healthy bout of alliteration: "The Shawnee sniper came through. We are speaking of Jimmy Thomson the big blaster of golf."[62] (Thomson was then based in Shawnee on the Delaware.) Interestingly, Thomson's prize of $2,100 and the overall purse of $7,500 were swelled by higher than expected gate receipts, as huge crowds attended the event. The practice of purses being boosted on an *ad hoc* basis such as this was not unusual during these years.

This year also saw a new private sponsor emerge. While Seagram distillers and *The Los Angeles Times* saw golf sponsorship as a worthwhile investment, generally it was local chambers of commerce that underwrote the tour. Goodall's, which manufactured the Palm Beach range of golf clothing, was a welcome "capture" for Fred Corcoran as a sponsor. The event used a highly complicated round-robin format involving only 15 selected players. Sam Snead won the tournament played at the Kenwood Country Club in Cincinnati, and with it the first prize of $1,000. Sam had to work hard for his money, though, as the pros played a total of 126 holes. Goodall's would remain a sponsor on the PGA tour until 1957.

The year 1938 also witnessed some serious first prizes

"The Chief," Ky Laffoon (courtesy Monte McNew).

on offer, even if the uneven distribution of money continued. For example, Jug McSpaden won the Miami Open and a $2,500 first prize. (In this event, the future PGA champion, Chick Harbert, won the amateur prize.) Later Ky Laffoon won the Cleveland Open and $3,000. In a decade of "characters," Laffoon was near the top of the list, but his eccentricities sometimes clouded the fact that he was a player of the highest class who was good enough to win the Radix Trophy for best scoring average of 1935. He also made the Ryder Cup team that year.

Laffoon was, however, a natural crowd pleaser who often dressed in a manner akin to Hagen. He was also deeply superstitious and regularly carried a rabbit's foot in his pocket during tournaments. Indeed, after his highly lucrative win in Cleveland, he claimed, "I've been unconscious for three days.... This is the most superstitious game there is. My wife bothers me. I thought about her twice today and missed two putts."[63] Mrs. Laffoon stayed in the clubhouse for the duration of the tournament.

The season's big winner, in every sense, however, was the now established Sam Snead, who won more than $19,000 in total, $5,000 of which came from winning a 108-hole tournament at Westchester. Snead also won the Vardon trophy for the best scoring average.

Among the more interesting happenings of that summer was the sight of two Walter Hagen's paired together at the St. Paul Open. By this time Hagen was 45 years old and had just finished yet another global tour. However, his presence and the novelty of seeing the original "Haig" paired with Walter Junior brought 5,000 spectators to the Keller Park course. Both men shot in the high seventies and missed the cut in a tournament won by Johnny Revolta.

The Masters was won by Henry Picard—a popular victory, as the "Chocolate Soldier" was well liked by both the press and his fellow

"The Chocolate Soldier" Henry Picard (courtesy Tufts Archives, Pinehurst, North Carolina).

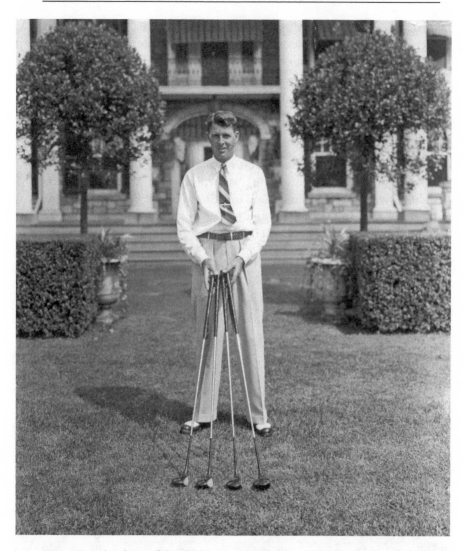

Henry Picard in front of the clubhouse at the Hershey Club. Originally, the building was the home of business magnate and philanthropist Milton Hershey, but he donated it to the club to help it develop during the Depression years (courtesy Hershey Community Archives, Hershey, Pennsylvania).

professionals. One reason for this was Picard's modesty: it was no surprise when, after his win at Augusta, he remembered the influence and encouragement of Walter Hagen back in 1931 when Picard was trying to break through. The pair were tied after regulation in the Carolina Open and Picard went on to beat Hagen by 10 shots in the play-off, 69 to 79. After the round Hagen sat Picard down and said, "Nice work kid ... you can be one of the greatest golfers in the world if you work hard on your game. Don't try to hit the ball so hard but keep working."[64]

The 1938 Masters, however, again showed the media's (and perhaps the public's) obsession with Bobby Jones, as evidenced in a report by the greatly respected Charles Bartlett. When reporting on Picard's win at the Masters, Bartlett appeared to adopt a populist approach when suggesting that "the happiest outcome of the tournament was the performance of one Robert Tyre Jones, Jr. of Atlanta, without whom there would be no Masters."[65] To call Jones' 16th place "the happiest outcome" when Picard had won would seem unfair, and would undoubtedly have embarrassed the ever-modest Jones. However, Jones still fascinated the American public, and perhaps Bartlett was merely responding to that fact.

Even more importantly, Bartlett went on to give an insight into *why* Picard won. This, suggested Bartlett, was partly due to him suffering "a bruised bone in the left thumb during the St. Augustine event," which "forced him to switch from an overlapping to an interlocking grip which left the ailing thumb free from pressure."[66] Many years later, Picard himself suggested that he actually hurt his thumb at the British Open, but the principle in Barlett's report was correct; Picard often confirmed that the grip change was significant and indeed he played with it for the rest of his life. Picard's winning score at Augusta was 285. As in the previous year, Ralph Guldahl lost out when he three putted the 70th and 72nd holes. Along with Harry Cooper, he finished two shots back.

Guldahl, however, gained revenge two months later, when he successfully defended his U.S. Open crown at Cherry Hills in Denver. This was the first time the championship was held west of Minneapolis. According to golf historian Tom Flaherty, the reason the USGA chose the relatively new Cherry Hills over the more established and prestigious Denver Country Club was because of its parking spaces and better practice facilities.[67] The parking space issue was certainly relevant, as 10,000 people were estimated to have watched on the final day, and for practice rounds up to 3,000 people attended. All of these were paying customers. Perhaps, as the Depression era was coming to a close, this turnout might have been expected for the nation's premier golf championship. However, it still represents evidence of how sports in general, and golf in particular, connected with the public and how important golf was as an escape route during these times.

Before the championship, two topics dominated: first, who would win, and second, the toughness of the Cherry Hills course, notably the narrow fairways. Regarding who would win, the prominent journalist Francis J. Powers gave defending champion Ralph Guldahl no chance. "About the only thing I am certain about," Powers wrote, "is that Guldahl will not repeat and the winner will be a fellow who has never held the championship."[68] Powers went on to suggest that Snead, who was runner-up the previous year, might go one better in 1938. Powers was wrong on both counts. Regarding the severity of the course, wise Harry Cooper said, "Well, I'll take 285 and wait for them to hand me the cup."[69] Harry proved to be a good judge, as Guldahl's winning score was 284, six shots better than the score for Dick Metz, whom he trailed by four entering the last round. Guldahl's final round of 69 was 10 better than that of Metz.

The 1938 National Open also provided a further insight into the pecking order as far as the priorities of golf writers and their newspapers during the Great Depression. As usual at U.S. Open time, the sports sections carried pages of reports and the event was often the dominant news item. Banner headlines, along with photos of Sarazen, Guldahl or Cooper, regularly featured and gave the game a wonderful prominence. Even practice rounds were watched and reported on with great interest. The U.S. Open also saw the featured writers appear, in contrast to many regular tour events where reports were often from the Associated Press. Most prominent among these was Grantland Rice.

The 1920s are often seen as a golden age in American sports journalism, with figures such as Damon Runyan and Paul Gallico coming to the fore. However, the 1930s were fortunate in that some of the craft's finest continued to have their say during the Depression years—and towering above them all was the figure of Grantland Rice. Rice first came to prominence in the early 1900s and remained the nation's leading and most highly paid sports writer for 50 years after. As well as demonstrating his journalistic prowess, which saw his sporting columns syndicated throughout the land, he had a long list of book titles to his name. Whether it was baseball or football, the Olympics, or boxing, Rice's narratives conveyed to the reader what all great sports writers do: a sense that "you were there." Rice also had an advantage no doubt earned through his skill and the respect in which he was held in the world of sport: he was friends with giants of the age such as Babe Ruth and Jack Dempsey. Grantland Rice also wrote a great deal on the game of golf and became a close friend of Bobby Jones. At Rice's funeral in 1954, Jones was a pallbearer, along with Jack Dempsey and Gene Tunney.

A feature of Rice's writing was that he often began or ended his reports with some of his own verse, such as this tribute to his friend Babe Ruth:

> I've seen a few who I thought could hit,
> Who fed the crowd on four-base rations,
> But you, Babe, are the Only It—
> The rest are merely imitations.[70]

Grantland Rice, the most influential of all golf writers (courtesy USGA).

Rice also regularly wrote about golf in verse, as in this observation of life for those on tour:

> With blistered calloused hands and feet
> With nerves that flutter down and up
> They wake at night in sudden fright
> To see a short putt rim the cup.[71]

Rice's style was part narrative, part poetic and part analytical. What was constant, however, was his ability to engage the reader with colorful phrases. For example, when reporting on Guldahl's win at Cherry Hills in 1938, Rice described the winner's final thrust as follows: "Starting four strokes back of Metz, the leader, big Guldahl, came down the stretch like a combination of Man O'War and War Admiral."[72] There were few sports fans in America who were not familiar with two of the nation's greatest ever racehorses, so the comparison between Guldahl and these two champions immediately created a powerful and easy-to-understand image for the reader.

Rice also had insight. In the same piece, he recorded how, "At the start of the final 18, I followed Metz, Hines and Guldahl in that order. The championship was here. I found both Metz and Hines tense and overkeen.... I swung back to Guldahl and suddenly came into an atmosphere of serenity and poise."[73] Guldahl shot a 69 to win comfortably.

Returning to Rice's capacity to make you feel as if you were there, it was, in part at least, because the writer himself *was* there. In the days long before TV screens and after-round press conferences, the writer had to find the story himself rather than wait for the player to give it to him. Therefore we learned of the "serenity and poise" of the winning Guldahl compared to Metz and Hines. Notwithstanding his abundant skill, only by seeing the golfers at close quarters could Rice give the reader the sense of the enormous pressure which goes with being in contention during the last round of a U.S. Open.

After his triumph at Cherry Hills, Guldahl traveled the well-worn exhibition route and cashed in on his second National Open victory. Claiming that his average annual tour earnings of $9,000 barely covered his expenses, Ralph explained that "the gravy comes from the sidelines."[74] In this regard, he embarked on a tour in which he played 45 exhibitions in 50 days in nine states.

Paul Runyan famously defeated Sam Snead by eight and seven in the PGA final this same year, despite being outdriven by 50 yards. In the build-up to the final, journalists focused on the contrasts between the two contestants and not just the differences in power. For example, Snead at this stage was noted for his sombre wardrobe while Runyan was something of a clothes horse who would soon be surpassed only by the flamboyant Jimmy Demaret. Henry McLemore also concentrated on the differing personalities, observing that "Snead is a newcomer; Runyan is a veteran. Snead is a loner who does not mix with his fellow professionals and would win no popularity contest in which his rivals voted. Runyan is a friendly mixer and very popular."[75] The Snead defeat at the hands of Runyan was interesting in other ways. In the immediate aftermath of the final, Sam admitted to being amazed by "Little Poison's" magic short game, which saw him complete the first 18 holes on the tough Shawnee course in 67 shots. However, a few months later Snead launched a scathing attack on match-play. The format, he said, was "foolish, meant nothing and was not a true test of skill." A number of pros agreed with Snead's verdict but some establishment figures strongly disapproved of what they saw as sour grapes. Former PGA and U.S. Open champion Olin Dutra, for example, had this to say: "Sammy hasn't learned to take his lickings as gracefully as he does his winnings. Speaking as a veteran pro, my guess is that the first time he wins a big match play tournament he will come out and say they are great."[76] Two-time PGA winner, Leo Diegel, also strongly disagreed with Snead. Snead clearly learned how to come to terms with the match-play format and went on to claim three PGA titles in his glittering career.

An important footnote to 1938 was that this year saw the first official tour victory of Ben Hogan when he accompanied the then more successful Vic Ghezzi to an emphatic victory in the Hershey Round Robin Fourball. Ben's share of the first prize was $1,100. In an early assessment of Hogan's famed intensity, Ghezzi remarked to Jimmy Demaret after the victory, "If we'd lost, I'm quite certain he would have jumped out of a window."[77]

The year 1939 saw a total of almost $200,000 on offer, with many substantial winners' checks being provided. Jimmy Demaret won the prestigious Los Angeles Open and $1,650, and Snead and Guldahl combined to win the Miami Fourball and $1,000 each. It was also a good year for Dick Metz, who, for example, won $1,000 for coming out on top at the Asheville Open, North Carolina. Metz was another colorful player from this era, with his dark, handsome and photogenic looks. Like Jimmy Thomson, Metz gained publicity when he married a Hollywood actress. In Metz's case it was Jean Chatburn, who appeared in many movies during the 1930s, notably *The Great Ziegfeld* starring William Powell and Myrna

Loy. However, Metz could also play golf, even if one newspaper named him "hard luck Hank"[78] because of his number of close misses. Some of this criticism was based on his surrendering a four-shot lead to Ralph Guldahl when finishing second in the 1938 U.S. Open at Cherry Hills. Metz shot a final round of 79 to Guldahl's 69, finishing six shots behind the winner. The newspaper's judgment was somewhat unfair, as coming close indicated a significant level of achievement. Furthermore, Metz encountered serious health problems and in 1939 was nominated for "best comeback" in an Associated Press poll for athletes. Overall, Metz won 10 PGA events, including eight during the late 1930s. His best year was 1939 when aside from his win at Asheville, he won three tournaments including the San Francisco Match-Play Open. In the 36-hole final, he showed his qualities when he came from behind to beat Horton Smith on the last green.

One of the big stories of 1939 was the form of the relatively new E.J. "Dutch" Harrison—also known as the "Arkansas Traveler" because he was from Little Rock, where he began golf as a caddie. Harrison was discovered by Horton Smith and for a time was his assistant in Illinois. Always good for a quote, Dutch liked to play up his "country boy" image in a manner not dissimilar to Sam Snead. For example, after winning the Texas Open, he was asked what he would do with the prize money. "That'll help to feed the hogs" was the reply.[79]

As well as having a quick turn of phrase, Harrison became another of the game's celebrated hustlers. On one occasion he had Herman Keiser dress up as a caddie and play as his partner in a big-money game. The unsuspecting opponents were amazed when this man in caddie's overalls shot 67 and helped Harrison clean up. Harrison's "caddie" would go on to win the Masters in 1946. In 1939, Harrison won the Crosby and $500 and also won $1,200 for his victory in the Texas Open. Second place here, and $700, went to Sam Byrd, another interesting figure who was on the tour at this time.

For a period prior to 1936, Byrd was Babe Ruth's understudy (and often roommate) with the New York Yankees. Baseball and golf enjoyed a form of symbiotic relationship in this era, as many of the game's star names, such as Ruth, George Earnshaw, and Jimmy Foxx, played a great deal of golf and were accomplished players. It seemed that the winter training camps in Florida, with lots of golf courses nearby, provided a natural home for the hitters and pitchers. Byrd began his golfing education as a caddie near his home in Birmingham and no less an expert than Tommy Armour tipped him as a future pro should he decide to switch from baseball. In fact, Byrd turned professional in 1936 and eventually became a tournament winner in the 1940s. Indeed, he lost out to Byron Nelson in the final of the 1945 PGA Championship. Byrd believed that many of the principles of the baseball "swing" could be applied to golf and he became a teacher of note later in his career. He is credited with giving the renowned instructor Jimmy Ballard his start in the teaching business.

One of the more interesting events that year was the New Orleans Open. The event was held during Mardi Gras and the prize fund of $10,000 was underwritten by the local mayor, Robert Maestri. Furthermore, admission was free and it was estimated that 32,000 people attended. In an unexpected bonus for the players, with rooms at a premium because of Mardi Gras, 32 professionals availed of the generosity of club members who made their homes available to their illustrious guests. Henry Picard won the $2,000 first prize, but just as importantly those finishing as far down as 20th place received $100.

New Orleans, however, was the exception and for the rest of the year the pattern reverted to type. At Scranton, for instance, Picard won again and received $1,200, with Nelson finishing 20th and receiving the last money on offer—$20. Similarly, Ralph Guldahl won the Dapper Dan in Pittsburgh and the considerable first prize of $2,500 after an 18-hole play-off with Sarazen and Shute. Here there were 30 cash prizes, the last of which was $8.33. The Dapper Dan was also significant as it once again showed the varied sources of sponsorship during the Depression years. In this case the tournament owed its existence to a sportsmen's club that was founded in 1936 by the sports editor of the *Pittsburgh Post-Gazette,* Al Abrams. The plan was to hold fund-raising dinners and sporting events, such as golf tournaments and boxing promotions, to raise money for charity. While there may have been certain tax advantages with this strategy,[80] in many ways it was an early example of the link between professional golf tournaments and charities which became so popular in future years. It is estimated that today's PGA tour raises $1 billion annually for charities. Incidentally, the name "Dapper Dan" came about because the original members of the sportsmen's club were always dressed in a dapper fashion.

A further note of interest concerning the Dapper Dan was the contribution of Horton Smith in his capacity as chairman of the Tournament Committee. Certainly there was little doubt that by this stage Fred Corcoran was the salesman regarding the tour. However, it was also clear that Smith was very much the "nuts and bolts" man when it came to the question of how tournaments should be run. In this regard, Smith wrote to Al Abrams well in advance of the Dapper Dan and advised him that "gallery control and gallery comfort are very important and, to my mind, are not handled properly one time out of ten." Smith also went on to tell Abrams that he liked "low round prizes and driving contests if properly organized."[81] As with his comments after the northwestern swing in 1936, these guidelines represented another example of the tour's growing professionalism, much of it driven by Smith. In the event, Abrams took Smith's advice and held a long driving contest, which was won by Pinehurst professional Ted Turner with a blow of 336 yards. For this feat Turner won $100, a not insignificant sum for the times.

A final note about the 1939 Dapper Dan: the role (and place) of professional golfer's wives was raised once again. The wives of those competing on the Grapefruit Circuit came from a wide range of backgrounds, such as Sunday School friend (Mrs. Byron Nelson), grand-daughter of

It was not unusual for the player's wives to do some knitting during tournaments. Here Byron Nelson helps his wife Louise. This photograph was taken in between matches at the 1938 PGA Championship at Shawnee-on-Delaware (courtesy USGA).

the president of the Singer Sewing Machine empire (Mrs. Horton Smith), and Hollywood divorcee (Mrs. Jimmy Thomson). Despite their diversity, many wives traveled with the "winter troupe" and supported their men in a variety of ways. Some preferred to knit in the clubhouse and wait for their husbands to finish their rounds, and others looked after the family finances on tour. On one occasion, Mrs. Wiffy Cox was seen holding a bucket of ice to her husband's head; this was during the unbearable heat at the U.S. Open of 1933 at North Shore. Mrs. Cooper followed her husband during tournaments but never wore green because of Harry's superstition, while Lawson Little's wife counted the number of putts he took and the couple discussed strategy after the round.[82] However, the wives' presence at tournaments was not universally welcomed.

Earlier in the decade the ever-quotable Gene Sarazen claimed that "the saddest thing in golf, it's those zealous, jealous and gossiping wives who haunt their husbands and watch them fire every shot in a money tournament.... It's time the shackled pros arose in a body and told them to stay home, watch their pro shops or sew buttons on the old man's shirts."[83] (His friend Tommy Armour claimed that "no other pro would have mentioned the subject without hiring a bodyguard armed with machine guns."[84]) Sarazen's view was particularly interesting as at this stage, his wife Mary was known to travel to some tournaments with her husband. On a lighter note, we saw how in 1937 Laverne Guldahl traveled to the Ryder Cup match in England to protect her handsome husband Ralph from the clutches of adoring women golf fans. However, there was also a more chauvinistic element to this story, as both Hagen and Sarazen felt that Laverne and the other wives who made the trip to England were something of a distraction to the main order of business.

In early 1939, when plans were made for the Ryder Cup match to be played later that year in America, Commander Roe, who was secretary of the British PGA, announced that no wives would be allowed to travel with the British team. "I have many objections to wives travelling with husbands to an international match and as long as I have anything to do with the PGA, the rule will be enforced," were Commander Roe's exact words.[85] The match was later canceled due to the outbreak of war but the issue of the role of wives did not disappear. And at the Dapper Dan, once again it was Gene Sarazen who made the headlines. "Sarazen Tells Wives to Stay at Home" read a banner headline in the *Pittsburgh Press*.[86] There was very little by way of support from Sarazen's fellow professionals, but the wives certainly came out in defense of their wishes (and rights) to travel with their husbands and if necessary to bring their children along.

Mrs. Ray Mangrum and Mrs. Lloyd Mangrum were said to have "chuck-
led" at the news. Alongside photographs of "Mrs. Byron Nelson" and
"Mrs. Ben Hogan" at the Dapper Dan, it was reported that "Mrs. Denny
Shute" was "her husband's principal moral support on the course, attrac-
tively dressed in a lavender cotton frock with matching hat, she watched
every stroke her husband made around the course."[87] In fact, Denny
claimed that his wife's presence on tour was a great help, as he let her do
the worrying while he concentrated on the shot in hand. As we saw earlier,
when Byron Nelson felt it was too expensive to bring his wife Louise on
"the Evergreen Trail" which took in Seattle and Canada, travel expenses
were always a concern. However, whenever possible it seems to have been
a burden that many were happy to carry, even in those difficult times.

The 1939 National Open was won by Byron Nelson and it proved
to be an incident-packed championship. Going into the event at Spring
Mill, Philadelphia, Ralph Guldahl was the hot favorite at 6/1 to complete
a hat trick of victories. Despite not being able to make it three in a row,
he put up a creditable showing and finished just four back. Those next
in the betting at 8/1 included Nelson and Snead. Also at 8/1 was Harry
Cooper, who was, as ever, the sentimental favorite to end his drought in
the majors. In the end, the championship was about four players—Snead,
Nelson, Wood and Shute—with history judging this to be the one that
Snead lost rather than being Nelson's first National Open win. This verdict came about because of Snead's infamous 8 at the par five 72nd hole
when a par would have won and a six would have seen him gain a play-
off. Snead later recalled that in the aftermath, he had been called "yellow
and a bum and a meathead." He also conceded that he lost almost 30
pounds due to the stress caused by the 72nd hole.[88] So much has been
written about Snead's blow-up that an extremely eventful play-off has
often been overlooked.

For example, after the scheduled 18-hole play-off, Nelson and Wood
were tied with excellent scores of 68 while Shute shot 76. Nelson had a
birdie four at the last to force the play-off. This necessitated another 18
holes, as USGA rules decreed that a "round of golf" must be played to
decide the outcome of its Open. This time Nelson shot 70 to Wood's 73,
helped greatly by an eagle two at the par four fourth hole, where he holed
out with a one iron. This stroke of luck was the subject of much debate
after the play-off, as it was yet another example of the jinx which appeared
to follow Wood in the majors. Indeed, Wood's wife rhetorically asked,
"It hardly seems fair, does it? I mean for a fellow to sink such a shot in a
playoff for a national championship. And it is always Craig who suffers

most."[89] As we shall see, however, Craig ended his jinx in spectacular fashion two years later. After his win, Nelson confirmed his standing as one of golf's nice guys when it was revealed that he gave his caddie Jim Fraleich $130 (more than the traditional 10 percent of the $1,000 winner's check), plus a brand new set of irons and a new pair of golf shoes. Even when allowing for the fact that the caddie had to go 108 holes, this represented a very decent gesture on Byron's part.

For Nelson's defeated opponent in the play-off, Craig Wood, this was yet another disappointment in major championships to rank alongside his play-off defeats to Shute at St. Andrews in 1933 and to Sarazen at Augusta in 1935. And he did not leave Spring Mill quietly. Before the play-off, PGA President George Jacobus went on the radio to declare his hope that Nelson would win. This may have been understandable, as the two were friends. As we know, Jacobus had hired Nelson as his assistant at Ridgewood and he acted as a mentor to the young Byron before he moved to Reading, the base from which he won at Spring Mill. However, with more than a little justification, Wood believed that as the president of the association which represented *all* professional golfers, Jacobus should not have shown any favoritism. "Things can never be the same between us" was his parting shot to Jacobus.[90]

Two months earlier at Augusta, Ralph Guldahl had won the Masters. He went into the tournament in great form, having won at Greensboro the previous week. Yet again, the crowds at Greensboro indicated the popularity of the tour, as a "crowd of 10,000 people saw Guldahl, Little, and the young home towner, Clayton Heafner, finish in the dusk in the same threesome to win the top three money prizes."[91] Never the most popular or modest of players, after this victory Guldahl announced that he expected to win the Masters. It will be recalled that in 1937, Guldahl lost six shots to Byron Nelson in two holes on the back nine of the last round. This time it was Ralph's turn, as his decisive final nine of 33 included an eagle at number 13 and a birdie at number 15. Standing on the final hole with a one-shot lead, he managed a solid par four at the uphill final hole courtesy of a drive, three iron and two putts from the fringe. Ninety minutes earlier, Snead had finished with a score of 280 and looked set for his first major title—but just as at Oakland Hills in 1937, Guldahl was just too good. His final total of 279, a new record, saw him beat Snead by one shot. At this time he was probably the world's best player, with three recent major wins and a host of tour victories. Indeed, some newspapers were even affording him the ultimate praise by calling him "the peer of Bobby Jones."

By now Guldahl's fame was at its peak and his success brought additional commercial rewards, with car manufacturer Studebaker being one of the most notable in this regard. Not long after his Masters win, Studebaker claimed that 15,000 of its "Champion" model, priced at $660, had been bought by dealers in anticipation of unprecedented demand. "I've long been sold on quality and performance," said Ralph, "so naturally when I wanted the tops in lower-price cars I picked the Studebaker Champion. It's got plenty of championship form and perfect followthrough." The advertisement even went on to say that "golf experts say Ralph Guldahl is heading for recognition as the world's greatest golfer."[92] Despite his less than colorful image, the tall Guldahl cut a handsome figure alongside his Studebaker. However, the win at Augusta turned out to be his final triumph in the majors; only a few years later the same newspapers were asking, "What happened to Guldahl?"

In the PGA Championship, Henry Picard won a thrilling final when

"Big" Ed Dudley, an elegant player and president of the PGA (courtesy Broadmoor, Colorado Springs).

he defeated Byron Nelson in the 36-hole final at Pomonok Country Club, New York. Picard was one down playing the 36th hole but squared the match. Then at the par four 37th hole, Henry found his drive was plugged having been run over by a truck. In those pre-televised golf days, golf fans relied on short Newsreel or Pathe News reports at local cinemas to see their heroes in action. However, in this instance the offending vehicle was a sound unit covering the extra holes drama for radio: the tournament one of the first events to be broadcast live on air. After receiving a free drop, Picard proceeded to birdie the hole for victory.

At Pomonok, despite the thrilling final, the real headlines were made before the championship began and concerned the ongoing tensions that existed between the stay-at-home professionals wing of the PGA and those who played on tour. As we know, the reality was that those who toured also had club jobs, but this group often felt that as box office draws, their contribution to the advancement of the game was not always fully recognized by the Association.

In this instance it seemed that two-time PGA winner Denny Shute was two days late in paying his $25 PGA dues. For this infraction, the PGA executive committee voted by eight to three to ban him from playing in the 1939 event. This decision provoked a powerful reaction from the professionals who, in a show of solidarity, threatened to strike. A petition was handed to the executive committee on the day of the tournament, reading: "We the undersigned players will refuse to play unless the executive committee of the PGA exercise their power by voting to admit Shute into the 1939 championship."[93] The undersigned group of about 50 players included Snead, Hagen, Guldahl, Picard, Nelson, and Sarazen.

This team of heavyweights made it clear to the PGA that it risked having no tournament in 1939. Ironically, it was PGA president and Bob Harlow's old nemesis, George Jacobus, who came to the rescue of the pros. In the past, Harlow and some of the leading professionals believed that Jacobus did not always pay enough attention to the star names who underpinned the tour. However, in this, his last year in office, Jacobus overruled the majority on the executive committee, led by Tom Walsh, and insisted that Shute must play. And so the championship went ahead. The tensions, however, did not end there. One member of the executive committee who supported the pros over the Shute incident was Ed Dudley, who was regarded by the touring professionals as one of their own. In this regard he had impeccable credentials, as he was a Ryder Cup player and a multitournament winner. He was also head professional at Augusta.

Unsurprisingly, those who played the circuit wanted Dudley to replace Jacobus as president of the PGA but he was defeated by Tom Walsh. A few years later, however, the pros got their wish and Ed was appointed president.

The Ryder Cup was scheduled to be held in Florida in November of that year. Hagen was again named captain of the American team, with Henry Cotton leading the British. However, the British PGA called off the matches in September due to the outbreak of war in Europe. While the abandonment of the Ryder Cup was inevitable once war was declared, from a golfing perspective it was a pity, as a war of words between Gene Sarazen and Henry Cotton had broken out earlier that year. Amid reports that Cotton and some other British professionals had refused to embark on an American tour without some substantial financial guarantees, Sarazen asked, "What's wrong with this British chap Cotton that he claims to be the world's best golfer but demands a guarantee before he will come over for some matches in this country." Reminding everyone that he, Hagen, Armour and Jones had regularly traveled to Britain to compete, Sarazen enquired, "Did we ask for a guarantee? Let Cotton and his friends come here and win some honor for their country."[94] Cotton responded by saying that he never claimed to be the world's best golfer but it seemed that the feelings toward Cotton (among some Americans at least), which surfaced in 1937, were still in evidence. Ironically, during the previous year Sarazen indicated he would not play in the 1939 Ryder Cup matches in protest at the fact that he was not named U.S. captain. His complaints were directed squarely at George Jacobus, who had the power to make such appointments. However, even without him, it would seem that the fans missed out on a more full-blooded contest than usual.

Thus the Ryder Cup matches in Britain were canceled due to the outbreak of war. Similarly, after 1939, the British Open Championship would not be held again until 1946. In a letter to PGA President Tom Walsh, Henry Cotton told of how in Britain, "Golf is just alive. Our courses are covered with posts, poles, trenches ... anything to stop airplanes having an easy landing."[95] However, with America not yet in the war, golf maintained its normalcy in the United States and the Grapefruit Circuit continued throughout 1940 with very little change, even if the total prize fund of almost $170,000 was somewhat down in 1939. There was one change, however, which dominated the sports pages—the supremacy on tour by golfers from the Lone Star State. "What is the remainder of the golfing world going to do about these Texas Rangers?" asked Grantland Rice.[96] The "Rangers" in question were primarily Demaret, Nelson and Hogan, who between them had 16 victories and who in different ways would dominate the year.

As usual, the Los Angeles Open was held in January, with the first prize of $1,500 taken home by Lawson Little. After some difficult years as a pro, this was an important victory for Little and undoubtedly contributed to him becoming National Open champion in June of that year. One of Jimmy Demaret's early wins was in the New Orleans Open. Held as usual around Mardi Gras time and with an "admission free" policy which ensured large crowds, New Orleans was one of the more attractive stops on tour. It also helped that the tournament boasted a $10,000 purse, with Demaret receiving $2,000 as the winner. This was one of the year's largest first prizes and contrasted sharply with the $700 Lloyd Mangrum got for winning at Thomasville and the $250 Nelson received for winning the Ohio Open.

It was at the always prestigious Western Open that Demaret really made his mark, but here some early headlines were made by Byron Nelson. As one of the game's gentlemen, it surprised many when, after a first round of 78 and an opening nine of 40 in his second round, he withdrew. For this he was severely criticized both in the media and by veteran professionals. By quitting, he joined an illustrious group who had walked out when things were going poorly: Snead at Pasadena in 1938; Armour, who walked out at Oakmont in 1936 when he needed two pars for a 90; and most famously a very young Bobby Jones, who tore up his card at St. Andrews in the British Open. To be fair to Nelson, he later claimed that he was coming down with flu.

As for the tournament itself, Demaret beat his good friend Toney Penna in a play-off. Penna was another of the Italian American professionals. While he had a successful playing career with four career wins, his security came from his association with the MacGregor Golf Company. As we saw earlier, it was not uncommon for leading players to sign up emerging stars such as Snead for the equipment company to which they were affiliated. In Penna's case, he was signed by MacGregor in 1934 to act as a golfing "emissary" on a salary of $500 per month—not bad money in the early 1930s, especially when it was guaranteed. His job was to play on tour and at each stop try to boost MacGregor sales with the club pro as well as to sign up promising players. In this regard, Penna signed up Ben Hogan for $250 in 1937 on the recommendation of Henry Picard. It was undoubtedly a "steal" for MacGregor, but at that stage of his career, $250 was very important to Hogan. Hogan would remain with MacGregor for many years. However, shortly before he went into the equipment business for himself, Hogan defied Penna by playing Titleist balls instead of the latest Tourney ball from MacGregor. When challenged by Penna at the practice tee in Augusta in 1952, Hogan told him that "MacGregor balls and equipment were junk."[97] That was more or less the end of Hogan's relationship with MacGregor. As for his relationship with Penna, there never really was one, as antagonism existed between the two men for years.

Demaret's win at the Western was part of a hot streak in which he won six times in 11 starts. One of these was the first of his three Masters wins. Before the tournament, much of the media attention again focused on Bobby Jones, who shot a 66 in practice to raise the hopes of his supporters. Unlike today, when players play two or three balls at each hole and do not necessarily "keep score," in the 1930s and 1940s practice rounds for the majors were closely watched by the public and the media. These rounds were seen as a guide as to where to put your money when the tournament proper started. Jones, however, did not feature prominently when the Masters began and instead Demaret won by four over fellow Texan Lloyd Mangrum with a score of 280, just one shot higher than Guldahl's record aggregate the previous year. In his last round of 71, Jimmy was a model of consistency with 17 pars and one birdie.

Ever since winning the Texas PGA title in 1934, Demaret had made steady progress on tour and enjoyed a win in each of the 1938 and 1939 seasons. More than that, he brought something fresh to the professional game and by 1940 his image as a colorful player was firmly imprinted in the minds of both the media and the public. Reports of him at the time rarely failed to mention his multicolored attire or the fact that he was always smiling. "If tournament golf," stated the *Miami News,* "had been sick for want of another Hagen—and that seems to the finding of every diagnostician—Jimmy Demaret is just what the doctor ordered."[98] This carefree image sometimes camouflaged just what a wonderful player Demaret was. Just as Denny Shute had forecast back in 1935 in his comments about players from Texas, Demaret learned to "hold" his shots in the windy conditions and firm ground of the Lone Star State. He served his apprenticeship with Jack Burke, Sr., who also taught him. Burke's son and two-time major winner Jackie Burke, Jr., always believed that Ben Hogan's power fade was influenced by Demaret, who developed the shot several years earlier.[99] Certainly Hogan is on record regarding how much he admired Jimmy's shot-making ability. In total, Demaret won 31 times on tour and was a regular on Ryder Cup teams.

The U.S. Open was held at Canterbury and appeared to have ended in a three-way tie when Lawson Little, Gene Sarazen and Ed "Porky" Oliver all finished at 287. However, Oliver, in the company of Johnny Bulla and Dutch Harrison, was disqualified for teeing off earlier than his allotted time to avoid bad weather. Naturally this story dominated the post–Open reports, and there were mutterings from both players and journalists about Hagen's propensity for occasionally teeing off late and

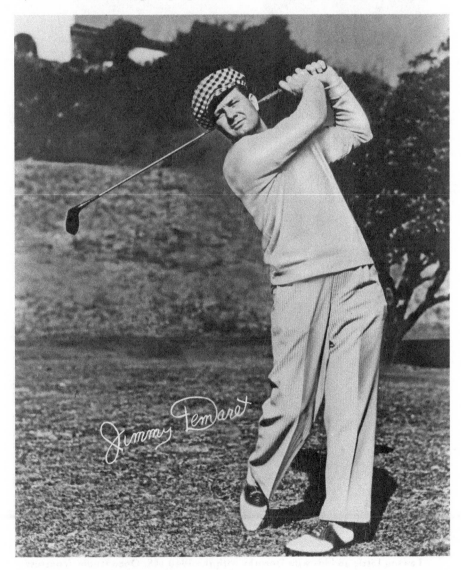

Jimmy Demaret, as always elegantly attired (courtesy USGA).

Lawson Little and his wife Dorothy with the 1940 U.S. Open trophy (courtesy USGA).

without penalty. Nevertheless, the USGA was adamant that Oliver had not checked in with the official starters and the ruling to disqualify him stood.

As for the winner, Lawson Little, not many people favored him. Indeed, after his triumph, journalist Henry McLemore claimed that the only two people who believed he could win were Little and his wife Dorothy.[100] Before the tournament, much of the build-up was centered on whether Sam Snead had recovered from his 72nd hole collapse at Spring Mill in the previous year and if Guldahl could make it three wins in four years. Prophetically, however, in the week preceding Canterbury, Little claimed that his game was in good shape. He also stated that the reason his professional career to date had not seen him fulfill expectations was because he spent too much time playing exhibitions for Spalding after 1936, which had left him drained. There was a certain irony here: when he turned pro in late 1935, Little stated that exhibitions and endorsements, rather than tournaments, would be his source of income. It seemed, however, that tournament golf interspersed with rest periods was the right formula.

In the play-off, there was little doubt who the crowd were cheering for—and it was not Little. As we saw earlier, Little's personality did not always endear him either to the fans or to his fellow professionals. One report claimed that "It was not a popular victory ... three fourths of them [the 3,000-strong gallery] were rooting their hearts out for Sarazen, the stocky veteran in knickers."[101] Despite this, Lawson prevailed and joined an elite group who won both his national professional and amateur titles. This should have been something of a turning point in Little's career but he won only three more times on tour and it is fair to say that as a professional, he probably never truly realized his enormous potential.

Ed Oliver's (the nickname "Porky" was bestowed because he weighed 240 pounds) disqualification continued to make the news after Canterbury, and he received a great deal of sympathy in the press and from his fellow professionals. However, he took full responsibility for his disqualification and did not allow his bad fortune to affect his golf. This was Oliver's rookie year and earlier on he won both the Crosby and the Phoenix Open. A few weeks after the U.S. Open, he won the St. Paul Open and a first prize of $1,600. St. Paul boasted one of the bigger purses in 1940, with 30th place taking home $50. Oliver went on to have a fine career featuring three Ryder Cup appearances and second-place finishes in the PGA, the National Open and the Masters.

Even though America was not yet in the war, there was no escaping it, with daily headlines of events in Europe and discussions regarding the ongoing question of whether America should or would become involved. At all levels of American society, fund-raising activities for the war effort were taking place. In this regard, the pros were "doing their bit" by way of fund-raising matches. One such initiative involved those selected for the canceled Ryder Cup match of 1939, versus a team led by Gene Sarazen. Gene was critical of the 1939 selection (he was omitted) and publicly declared he could find a team to beat the chosen few. His challenge was accepted and the match was held over two days at the tough Oakland Hills course, with the Ryder Cup team being captained by (who else?) Walter Hagen. Gene's team included Demaret, Hogan, and Little, while Nelson, Picard and Snead were among those who Played for Hagen. In the end the Ryder Cup team of 1939 maintained their honor with a 7–5 win in front of large crowds. More importantly, $16,000 was raised for the Red Cross. In addition to this effort, the PGA set aside a few weeks in the summer to raise funds for the war effort. This involved many top players, such as Horton Smith and Jimmy Thomson, foregoing the possibility of lucrative exhibitions in favor of charity professional–amateur events or fourball matches. Including the $16,000 from the match between the Ryder Cuppers and Sarazen's team, a total of $50,000 was raised.

The fund-raising drive for the war effort was very much instigated by Fred Corcoran and by Tom Walsh, the PGA president who had replaced George Jacobus in 1939. What these two men also initiated, in the summer of 1940, were plans to start a PGA Hall of Fame. Baseball started its "Hall" in 1939 and both Walsh and Corcoran were anxious that golf should also have its way of formally honoring those who had made a significant contribution to the game. The Hall of Fame began the following year, with Jones, Sarazen, Hagen and Ouimet being the first inductees.

The year's final major was the PGA, which was held that year at the Hershey club. As the title holder and resident pro, Henry Picard was the strong favorite. Sam Snead was also in the news, with questions again being asked about his ability to win a major golf title. Ever since his final hole collapse at the previous year's National Open, the "hexed hillbilly" tag had followed Snead around. In the event, however, there was a great deal of admiration for Sam's performance at Hershey as he battled through to the final to play Byron Nelson. And here, unlike his previous PGA final appearance when he was thrashed by the diminutive Paul Runyan, Sam fought back from a two-hole deficit after the first 18 holes to take a one-up lead with three to play. Byron, however, birdied two of the last three holes to win. Nelson's prize was $1,100, which was considerably less than Porky Oliver's prize at St. Paul, but of course Byron would gain from manufacturer's bonuses and exhibition fees.

A few weeks later Snead gained a form of compensation when he beat Nelson into second place in the Anthracite Open. As the name suggests, this tournament was held in the nation's major coal region, Scranton, Pennsylvania, and coal figured in the prizes. First, as was often the case in these times, there was a long driving contest before the tournament began. This was won by big-hitting Jimmy Thomson, whose three drives averaged almost 300 yards. For this success, Jimmy won a ton of coal delivered to his home. Second, whoever shot the low round each day received the same prize. Third, in addition to his first money of $1,200, Sam received a ton of coal prepaid to his home. These imaginative prizes, just before the onset of winter, were not insignificant during these times.[102]

As the year wound down, the final event was one of the more attractive and lucrative stops on tour, the Miami Open in December. Staged at the luxurious Biltmore complex, the tournament offered good weather, a touch of glamour, and a purse of $10,000. The tournament was also well attended, with 17,000 coming through the gates. Here Nelson completed a wonderful year by taking the first prize of $2,500. The glamour was provided by the Duke and Duchess of Windsor, who were staying at the Biltmore for a few days while the Duchess was recovering from a tooth infection. It was recorded that 27 pieces of luggage came in advance of the couple and that the Duke, a keen golfer, regretted he would be unable to watch some of the play in the Miami Open.[103] However, the Duke did find some time for golf when just after the tournament ended, he played an exhibition with a group which included Snead and Sarazen. Snead shot a 65 while the Duke had a respectable 88. "Eddie Plays Golf; Watches Snead Score Amazing 65" read a headline in the local *St. Petersburg Times.* During his visit, the Duke, who was also governor of the Bahamas, promised to sponsor an exhibition match for the Red Cross in Nassau the following spring. The Duke was true to his word: in March 1941 he refereed a match in which Jones and and Armour beat Hagen and Sarazen; $7,000 was raised for the Red Cross.

Two other titles were decided in Miami: leading money winner and winner of the Vardon Trophy for the year's best scoring average. Ben Hogan (or "Benny," as he was often called then) captured both. Even though he did not win a major, 1940 was Ben Hogan's breakthrough year and was the real start of his ascent to the very top of the game. It was also

"Bantam" Ben Hogan in action (courtesy Tufts Archives, Pinehurst, North Carolina).

the culmination of his on-and-off 10-year journey to this point in his career, which has been recorded so eloquently by Gene Gregston, Curt Sampson and Hogan's authorized biographer James Dodson. Starting in Texas in 1930, his career to date had been littered with disappointments, ranging from having the tires stolen from his car on his way to a tournament, to working as a bellhop in a hotel, to dealing cards in a casino. Hogan also held some poorly paid jobs at nonprestigious golf clubs where he tried to eke out a living selling balls and giving lessons. He did not enjoy teaching but as he often recalled later in life, the paucity of business in these clubs had the advantage of leaving him plenty of time for this favorite past-time: practicing. All of these undertakings were part of his quest to get on the tour and stay there. As we saw earlier, Henry Picard eased his mind considerably with his offer of financial backing and by the end of the 1930s there were clear indications that both Hogan's game and his state of mind were in very good shape.

This was certainly the case in 1940, when Hogan had four victories in which he produced some sensational scoring. Three of his wins—at Pinehurst, Greensboro, and Asheville—came within the space of a few weeks, and his combined score for these wins was 34 under par. He also produced a number of high finishes and this consistency saw him beat his fellow Texans, Nelson and Demaret, for the scoring and money honors. For the record, Hogan won $10,655 in 1940, roughly $1,000 more than Nelson. At the end of the year he declared his satisfaction with his achievements but eschewed any talk of him being the number one golfer. He stated, "I never want to reach the top.... There is only one way he can go from there and that's down." He also went on to say that "Nelson is tops."[104] Hogan may have been trying to take the pressure off himself and factually he was correct, as Nelson had already won three majors compared to none for Hogan. In addition, earlier in 1940, Nelson beat Hogan in a play-off for the Texas Open. However, considering his later obsession with passing Nelson and with being number one, these were interesting comments to make at this stage of Hogan's career.

With Hogan, Nelson, and Demaret, finishing one, two, and three in the money list, the question raised by Grantland Rice about Texas supremacy was a constant theme during the year. Based on first-hand experience, Jimmy Demaret believed that Texas was a very competitive environment in which to learn your golf. In local events, either amateur or professional, only the best survived. Tournament director Fred Corcoran, in contrast, believed this success came because of a new shot which the Texans had developed. "They call it the push shot ... it travels in a low arc, not very far off the ground and it's wonderful for distance."[105] Corcoran may have erred in suggesting the push shot was new, as a young Bobby Jones recalled trying (unsuccessfully, he admitted) to learn the same shot from an article by Harry Vardon. As Jones described the shot, it was "to be played with a minimum of hand action, striking the ball a sharply descending blow and sending it on a low trajectory towards the green."[106] Regardless of whether the shot was new, there is little doubt that at the start of the 1940s, the Texas Rangers set new standards in regard to ball striking, just as Denny Shute had predicted.

Despite the Great Depression, the newspapers did their best to present an image of plenty with their headlines for tour events. "Pros Hit the Gold Trail" would be a typical sample. Naturally, this image suited sponsors looking for publicity. It also suited Bob Harlow and Fred Corcoran in their attempts to boost the image of the tour. However, as we have seen, the large total purse, or indeed first prize, often camouflaged the inequitable distribution of prize money. Special additional prizes, such as coal for a long driving contest in Pennsylvania, or bonuses, such as a box of oranges on the tee in Florida, were always welcome. Against this often uncertain background, it was not a major surprise that the big names such as Sarazen and Hagen spent much of the decade on exhibition tours abroad. Nor was it a surprise that almost all professionals were anxious to have a secure club job. Certainly, a look at the annual money lists helps illustrate the point. In 1934, for example, Paul Runyan led the way with $6,679, but to earn this amount he had to play in 21 events—an average of $318 per event. Similarly, in 1935, Johnny Revolta led the annual prize list with $9,543 from 34 events—an average of $278 per tournament. Considering that weekly expenses were generally $100–$150 and the circuit ran for approximately half the year, it is clear that even the most successful of players found it difficult to survive on tournaments alone. As Ralph Guldahl said, the "gravy" came from exhibitions, not to mention manufacturer's bonuses and advertising fees for the winners.

To be sure, toward the end of the decade there was more money on offer. In 1938, for example, Snead won the (then) enormous sum of $19,389. However, this was an exceptional year and twice the amount won by runner-up Johnny Revolta. In the same year, three-time major winner Denny Shute won just under $2,000. Despite a great deal of progress, increased publicity, and more prize money, the tour offered no guarantees as the Great Depression drew to a close. However, these harsh realities should not take away from the progress made by the tour during this decade, both on and off the course.

In September 1937, Spokane in the Pacific Northwest was preparing for a visit of President Roosevelt to celebrate one of the New Deal's greatest symbols, the Grand Coolee Dam. The dam would become one of the world's greatest producers of hydro-electricity and became globally famous after Woody Guthrie wrote his song "The Big Grand Coolee Dam." The local *Spokane Chronicle* had banner headlines on its front page highlighting FDR's visit. However, what was also notable was the presence on page 1 of a large and elegant hand drawing of Ralph Guldahl, who the previous day had defeated Horton Smith in an 18-hole play-off for the prestigious Western Open title, and who was the reigning National Open champion. In many ways the sight of the National Open champion sharing a front page with FDR symbolized the ongoing development of the professional game during the Great Depression.[107]

Epilogue

"This week all the world could see to what a well-chewed pulp golf's famed grapefruit circuit had been reduced."[1]—*Time* magazine, looking ahead to the extensively reduced 1943 tour

There is no agreed date as to when the Great Depression ended as, despite the immensely positive impact of the New Deal, the country experienced the occasional economic slump, such as the recession of 1937. What is not in doubt, however, is that the Pearl Harbor attacks of December 1941 saw the country mobilized for battle and a huge increase in the production of planes, tanks and the general arsenal of war. Full employment was now the norm in America.

For the game of golf in general, the war brought some changes, notably in regard to golf balls. With rubber at a premium, reconditioned balls became the norm and in the best American entrepreneurial traditions, the manufacturers were quick to respond. For example, in 1942 Spalding launched a range of "War Flite" reconditioned balls, with the "Bomber" model selling at $6 per dozen. As for the Grapefruit Circuit, little changed and tournaments were held regularly. Nineteen forty-one was the most normal of the war years, with many tournaments in place and the three majors being held. In contrast, the National Open was not held between 1942 and 1945. This is the official USGA version of events, although many believed that the Hale America tournament of 1942 was in effect the National Open championship. Ben Hogan certainly did: as the winner at the Ridgemoor Club, Chicago, he proclaimed, "If this wasn't an Open championship I don't know what could be."[2] Many newspapers agreed with him and referred to the win as his breakthrough in the majors. And Dan Jenkins, a Hogan friend and admirer and a vastly respected writer, always claimed this was indeed a U.S. Open. Neverthe-less, the USGA never recognized Hogan's win; if it had, Hogan would hold the record of five U.S. Open titles.

Nor was the Masters held between 1943 and 1945. Indeed, cows grazed at Augusta, and the Forest Hills Hotel, where many golfers and journalists stayed for Masters week, was taken over by the army as the Oliver General Hospital. However, the PGA Championship went missing only in 1943, and apart from this particular year, the tour itself endured remarkably well.

What changed from the start of 1942 was the make-up of the fields, as many of the leading players joined the forces. On occasion, Fred Cor-coran complained that it was difficult to find both sponsors and host clubs for tournaments, when so many of the name players were absent. Included in those who could not always play were Sam Snead, Paul Run-yan and Jimmy Demaret of the Navy, and Dutch Harrison and Vic Ghezzi of the Army. Lieutenant Horton Smith of the Army Air Force spent some time overseas but in his training base at Miami Beach he regularly played golf with Private (later Lieutenant) Ben Hogan, who was also stationed there. Ed Oliver was also drafted and on occasions represented the Army team. A shortage of gasoline was also a problem—even when players were available, rationing sometimes made trips to tournament venues impossible.

A number of players were excluded from the draft on health grounds, notably Byron Nelson and Jug McSpaden. These players, however, did contribute to the war effort, with both raising considerable sums by play-ing exhibitions. For some, it appeared wrong that a "leisure activity" con-tinued when the country was at war and when more pressing issues such as a shortage of gasoline often dominated the domestic news. Craig Wood, who was too old to be drafted, articulated the views of many when, in 1942, he declared, "I am not going to play in any winter tournaments. I am older than most people think and would not be drafted, no doubt, but I am not going to be seen carrying a bag of clubs about playing for high prizes when so many of our men are fighting the Huns and the Japs."[3]

However, the PGA (backed by a large body of public and media opinion) felt that maintaining morale, and fund-raising through golf, jus-tified the sense of normalcy which prevailed in the professional game. Indeed, the game received the ultimate imprimatur from the president. FDR, just as he had believed that leisure would help restore morale during the Depression years, suggested that the war effort would "be actually improved by sensible participation in healthful pursuits."[4]

In regard to fund-raising, apart from exhibitions, the PGA, led by Fred Corcoran, contributed significantly, notably by ensuring that the gate receipts for tournaments were often used for the benefit of war veterans. In one such instance, $20,000 was raised from the 1944 Texas Open and used to build a golf course for veterans at Ashburn General Hospital, McKinney, Texas.[5] On another occasion, $18,000 was raised for the general war effort when a "Ryder Cup" team captained by Hagen played a team of challengers which included Bobby Jones. In his match, Jones defeated Henry Picard 2/1. Even the majors contributed: in 1944, when the PGA Championship was held at Spokane, Washington, the local Athletic Round Table (ART) underwrote the championship's costs. The ART was extremely active in the area and had already brought a number of amateur golf events to the Northwest. On one occasion it had even sent a single club to a soldier serving in the Solomon Islands. It seems the serviceman had a dozen golf balls but nothing else.[6] After the PGA Championship concluded, it was estimated that a sum of $30,000 was donated to the Fort George Wright AAF Convalescent Centre and the Baxter General Hospital.[7] As for the tournament, Bob Hamilton caused a major upset by beating Byron Nelson in the final.

One semi-retired player also helped the war effort. It will be recalled that double major winner, Olin Dutra, left the tour in the mid- to late 1930s for the security of a club job at Wilshire, in his native California. Dutra remained at the club until 1945. In 1944, however, he persuaded both sponsors and the Wilshire club committee to host the Los Angeles Open at the club and $8,000 was raised in War Bonds and stamps. Jug McSpaden was the victor.[8]

Overall, apart from 1943 (when there were hardly any events), tournaments were held on a regular basis, with Nelson, McSpaden, et al. competing regularly; when Snead, Smith, Hogan and company could get leave, they also played. "Leave" certainly played a part as when Sgt. Dutch Harrison, who came to prominence at the end of the Depression years, gained passes from his army base in Dayton, Ohio, to win both the Charlotte and Miami Opens of 1944. In general, Nelson and McSpaden were by far the most prolific money winners, but this was the period when Hogan also became a regular tour winner, despite being in the services. In 1942, for example, Hogan gained enough leave to achieve five victories. Also, when Snead was on leave, he confirmed the class he showed in the late 1930s by finally winning his first major, the PGA title in 1942, and

"The Blonde Bomber" Craig Wood (courtesy Winged Foot Golf Club).

achieving several other wins during the war years. By and large, this period represented something of a "changing of the guard" as many key figures from the Depression era were no longer prominent.

Certainly Craig Wood, the man who lost out to Sarazen's albatross at Augusta and Nelson's holing a one iron at Spring Mill, achieved his "destiny" in 1941 with his wins in the National Open and the Masters. Approaching 40, by now the "Blonde Bomber" was seen as a veteran and his two major wins were very popular with both the public and the media. Indeed, the press named him "comeback athlete of the year." However, during America's war years, he achieved only one victory—at the Canadian Open of 1944. This would be his last victory on tour. Henry Picard "retired" from the tour at the end of 1942, but by 1944 was planning a comeback. While December 1945 saw him win the Miami Open and a prize of $2,250, this was a last tournament hurrah for "the Hershey Hurricane." Jimmy Thomson continued to play but achieved no wins after the 1930s. Jimmy did, however, make a movie with Ronald Reagan and Jane Wyman titled *Shoot Yourself Some Golf.* In this movie, Jimmy was the instructor while the future president and his then-wife were the enthusiastic learners. Harry Cooper did not manage a victory of note during these years. Neither did Denny Shute, a multiple major winner during the Great Depression, although Denny had some good finishes, such as being second to Nelson at Phoenix during Lord Byron's famous streak year of 1945.

Most noticeable of all, perhaps, was the regression of Ralph Guldahl, who went from being probably the best in the world in the late 1930s to being just another player in the 1940s. Guldahl won twice in 1940 but those were his last wins on tour. Ralph's slump was well publicized and many theories were advanced in an attempt to explain his decline. One centered on his book *Groove Your Golf,* which Ralph claimed to have written without any help from a ghost writer. The book was based on question-and-answer sessions Ralph gave when holding clinics on his exhibition tours. The theory went that during and after writing the book, Ralph started to think too much about his own swing and so lost his natural and individualistic way of playing the game.

Also noticeable was his tendency to play slowly. Guldahl had always been a methodical player but, perhaps because of his lack of form, he became even more deliberate. In one tournament in 1941, the somewhat volatile Johnny Bulla walked off the course, claiming that he would "rather never win a tournament than play with Guldahl."[9] The feud did not end there: later that year, in the Inverness Round Robin fourball match-play event, the pair were drawn to play against each other. This time, Bulla requested a referee with a stop watch. This turned out to be Fred Corcoran, who said, "I guess I'm stuck with the job of refereeing the match but I'd rather have Jack Dempsey in my place."[10] The "slow play" accusations just added to the picture of a one-time champion in decline. Guldahl dropped off the tour for a time but attempted a comeback in 1948, claiming that a hip ailment, which he said led to his decline, was now better. However, despite some impressive rounds, newspaper reports tended to focus on what he *had* achieved during his glory days, and not on what he was capable of doing in the present.

Double Masters champion Horton Smith won twice in 1941. When he was in the Army Air Force, Horton believed that the fitness program he underwent there would add another 10 years to his career. However, despite some good performances, the two victories in 1941 proved to be his final wins on tour. And while the 1935 PGA champion Johnny Revolta did win the Texas Open of 1944, his best years also belonged to the 1930s. Whether it was through age or loss of form, "the Winter Troupe" had now been largely replaced by a new wave.

This book has endeavored to discover how and why the professional golf tour of the 1930s evolved and even thrived when so many factors were apparently against it. Certainly, there were social factors. First was the fact that the game itself had become immensely popular in the previous decade; it seems that despite many difficulties, this popularity endured during the 1930s. Second, more people were playing the game (often on WPA-funded public courses). When these factors are combined, it becomes clear that there was an enthusiasm and an audience for professional golf. This audience was evidenced by the examples provided earlier of the large numbers who attended tournaments and exhibition matches. For example, the final day of the U.S. Open regularly saw crowds of 10,000, with practice days attracting 3,000-strong galleries. We also know that galleries of between 5,000 and 10,000 were not unusual for regular tour events and on occasions, such as the 1940 Miami Open, up to 17,000 attended. The New Orleans Open of 1939 attracted crowds of 32,000 and the "Spalding Fourball" drew 300,000 spectators nationwide during the few years of its existence. Even though admission was free for both of these events, these figures are further proof of the public's interest in professional golf and how the game grew during these years.

In regard to my earlier suggestion that the Grapefruit Circuit did not have one outstanding "draw," it is fair to suggest that for many golf historians and scribes, the 1930s represent something of a hiatus in the exciting history of American golf. Bobby Jones's retirement in 1930 signaled the end of a golden decade but as noted earlier, he continued to frequent the sports pages by virtue of his commercial activities. Advertisements highlighting his signature Spalding irons, for example, were often more prominent in golf magazines than any ads featuring the leading professionals. And, of course, there was also the Masters—*his* Masters—which commanded great attention regarding Jones's "comeback" in the inaugural event of 1934 and simply because of his association with what became golf's fourth major. Even though the triumvirate of Nelson, Snead, and Hogan came to prominence during the later Depression years, their names were more associated with the 1940s and, for Hogan especially, the 1950s.

And yet to suggest that the professional game in the Depression era did not represent a significant and at times memorable period in the history of American golf would not fit with the facts. Sarazen won four majors in the 1930s. Also, even if Hagen's major victories were behind him, he still won the occasional tournament and wherever he played was "box office gold." However, these players played sporadically during the Great Depression. In many ways, it was those whom history has often judged to be "lesser players" who counted most during the decade—for example, players such as multiple major winners Ralph Guldahl, Henry Picard, and Denny Shute, as well as regular tournament and Vardon Trophy winners like Harry Cooper. There were also the crowd pleasers such as the "Big Blaster," Jimmy Thomson, and the colorful Ky Laffoon. By virtue of their skill and their constant presence, these players literally kept the show on the road during these difficult times.

Of course, the tour needed backers. What was notable about the 1930s was that despite all the harsh economic realities of the times, a variety of sponsors saw sponsoring golf tournaments as a viable proposition for promoting their products, cities, or causes. These included a distiller, local chambers of commerce, newspapers, and charity organizers. Alongside this, equipment manufacturers such as True Temper, Wilson, Spalding, and MacGregor saw how leading players could enhance their products and attract new converts to the game, warrenting their ongoing investment in the tour and its players. Furthermore, it is clear that major manufacturers and suppliers of non-golfing products saw members of the Grapefruit Circuit as personalities who could sell their goods. These products ranged from Irish whiskey to Camel cigarettes to Wheaties breakfast cereal.

As for the tour itself, despite the internal politics, the decade saw a considerable amount of progress, notably with the introduction of a greater degree of professionalism and organization *and* the geographical expansion of the tour. Without doubt, the seeds of today's all-year-round tour were sown during this decade. Much of this progress was due to the combined efforts of Bob Harlow and Fred Corcoran (aided by Horton Smith). It might be stretching the facts to suggest that Harlow and Corcoran were comparable to Mark McCormack in terms of their capacity to see golf's commercial possibilities, both for individual players and for the tour. Nevertheless, both were pioneers who "sold" golf to the media, the public, and potential sponsors. Both are owed an immense debt by the professional game.

Selling the game to the newspapers was indeed important but as we have also noted, the print media clearly saw the game as worthy of promotion and as being important in terms of circulation. Certainly, coverage of golf varied depending on whether it was the National Open or a more low-key event with a $3,000 purse. The game also had to compete for column inches with the national sports of baseball and football. However, there is little doubt that overall the profile of the professional game, the tour, and its leading players was enhanced during the Depression years. The print media can take a great deal of credit for this, notably giants of the craft such as Grantland Rice, William D. Richardson and Charles Bartlett.

When discussions take place as to which golfers made the greatest contribution to the health of professional tournament golf (certainly in the pre–Tiger era), two names invariably stand out: Walter Hagen and Arnold Palmer. Compelling cases can be made for both. First, Hagen, whose skill and fighting spirit led him to 11 major victories, often when the odds were stacked heavily against him. Perhaps even more significant, however, was his off-course courage, which saw him rail against the snobberies (on both sides of the Atlantic) that pervaded the game at that time. The sheer force of his personality broke down many of the existing barriers and elevated the image of the professional golfer.

Second, Palmer, whose rise to stardom either coincided with the growth of televised golf or was the reason television networks became so interested in the game. Whichever theory we choose, there is no doubt that Palmer's personality and attacking style helped popularize the game, notably in the 1960s and, by extension, for decades after. It is one of the game's more pleasing facts that a healthy friendship and respect existed between these two men.

However, it is also important to see the history of professional golf in the United States as an ongoing work, with each generation passing on something worthwhile to the next. In this regard, and given the economic crisis faced by the country during the Great Depression, the names of Harlow, Corcoran, Guldahl, Runyan, Dutra, Revolta, Smith, Shute, et al. undoubtedly helped make the professional game better and left a significant legacy. Their contribution to the game deserves to be recognized accordingly.

Biographical Notes
on Players

Tommy Armour (September 24, 1894–September 11, 1968)

Like Walter Hagen, Tommy Armour's best years may have been behind him during the Depression era but he remained a wonderful player. He was born in Edinburgh and fought in World War I, where he received injuries which caused him to lose the sight in his left eye. After a successful amateur career he emigrated to America where, with some help from Walter Hagen, he became secretary at the prestigious Westchester-Biltmore Club. He and Hagen became lifelong friends. After turning professional, Armour built up a wonderful record which included 25 tour titles. Eight of these were won during the Depression years. Also, before the Masters began in 1934, he won the "professional grand slam" with a victory in each of the British Open, the U.S. Open, and the PGA Championship.

After 1935, Armour devoted more and more time to teaching and became perhaps the game's most famous instructor, notably at Boca Raton in the winter and at Winged Foot in the summer. Along with Herb Graffis, he wrote the best-selling instruction book, *How to Play Your Best Golf All the Time*. Armour died in New York in 1968 just a few weeks short of his 74th birthday. He was inducted into the World Golf Hall of Fame three years later. His grandson, Tommy Armour III, is a two-time winner on the PGA tour.

Billy Burke (December 14, 1902–April 19, 1972)

Billy Burke was born in Connecticut to a Lithuanian family who changed their name from Burkowski upon settling in America. He traveled the traditional caddie route into the game. His stellar year was 1931, when he won the U.S. Open after a play-off with George Von Elm. Both players made history as the play-off lasted 72 holes, the longest in history. In addition, 1931 saw Burke win four other events as well as make the Ryder Cup team. He also made the team in 1933. In total, he had 13 wins on tour and he finished third in the Masters on two occasions.

Like many players from that era, Burke combined playing with club duties; he spent 29 years at the Country Club, Cleveland. In recognition of his services to golf he was inducted into the Cleveland Sports Hall of Fame in 1984. He was also attached to the Clearwater Club, Florida, as a winter professional, before retiring in 1962. Billy Burke died in 1972 after a long illness.

Harry Cooper (August 6, 1904–October 17, 2000)

Harry Cooper was born in England but his parents emigrated to Canada when he was eight. From there his family moved south and eventually settled in Texas, where his father became a professional in Dallas. Interestingly for that time, Cooper's mother also taught golf. Like many other players from this era, he learned his golf in the tough conditions of Texas. Harry Cooper was known as the "nearly" man of golf because of his number of close calls in the majors. In the U.S. Open alone, he had seven top 10 finishes. However, he had a wonderful record and overall he won 31 tournaments, including prestigious events such as the Western Open. In 1937, he was the first recipient of the Vardon Trophy for best scoring average and the only reason he was not a Ryder Cup player was because he was born in Britain.

A nonconformist, unlike most pros Cooper did not always hold down a club job. Even so, between 1953 and 1978 he worked at the Metropolis Club in White Plains, New York. At the age of 93, he was still teaching at the Westchester Country Club. Cooper was inducted into the World Golf Hall of Fame in 1992 and he died in New York in 2000.

Fred Corcoran (April 4, 1905–June 23, 1977)

Along with Bob Harlow, Fred Corcoran was one of the first golf promoters. Like many of the pros, he started life as a caddie and progressed to becoming an administrator and then a PGA tournament manager in 1937. His daughter, Judy, wrote his biography and called it *Fred Corcoran: The Man Who Sold Golf*—and that is just what he did with the tour, the LPGA tour (which he helped to found) and the Canada Cup (later the World Cup). Helping the game grow internationally was very important to Corcoran and he liked to joke that he three-putted in 48 countries.

Among his other achievements was making golf for the partially sighted more accessible. To this day, the Corcoran Cup is played annually; it has raised millions of dollars for the charity, Guiding Eyes for the Blind. In 1975, Fred Corcoran was elected to the World Golf Hall of Fame— the first nonplayer to receive this award. Up to the year of his death in 1977, he remained involved in the game as tournament director of the Westchester Classic.

Wilfred Hiram "Wiffy" Cox (October 27, 1896– February 20, 1969)

Wiffy Cox came from Brooklyn and learned the game as a caddie at Westchester. He was known for his fiery temper but was also a fine player who claimed four victories in 1931, his best year on tour. In the majors, his best finish was tied for third in the 1934 U.S. Open, two shots behind the winner, Olin Dutra. In total he had nine victories on tour. He was a Ryder Cup player in 1931, when he achieved a 100 percent record in the two matches he played in.

In 1938, Cox landed the prestigious job of head professional at the Congressional Club in Washington, D.C. For a period, Congressional was taken over by the Office of Strategic Services (OSS) during World War II, and Cox was attached to the Hempstead Club on Long Island. Apart from that interval, Cox remained in his position until 1969, when he died from cancer. He played golf almost up to his death.

Tom Creavy (February 3, 1911–March 3, 1979)

Tom Creavy was born in Tuckahoe, Westchester County, and along with his brothers he learned the game by caddying. His proficiency at the game was evident from an early age. At 15, he won the Westchester County Caddie Championship. After turning professional he made a name for himself locally. It was in 1931 that he came to national prominence, when he won the PGA title. Despite many fine rounds and high finishes, this was his only victory. His career was also plagued by ill health in the form of spinal meningitis. Indeed, in 1943, an exhibition match was held to raise funds for him. Included in the fourball were Gene Sarazen and Byron Nelson. A sum of $2,000 was raised.

In later years Creavy became active in the Northeastern New York PGA and was elected president in 1957. The Association further honored him in 1977, when he was inducted into its Hall of Fame. He also taught a great deal and was head professional at the Saratoga Spa Club, New York, for 25 years. He died in Florida in 1979.

Jimmy Demaret (March 29, 1912–December 28, 1983)

Jimmy Demaret was another player of this era to emerge from Texas. He learned the game by caddying and more particularly when he became assistant to Jack Burke, Sr., at the River Oaks club in Houston. Apart from his sartorial elegance, Demaret was known for his strength and his low ball flight, which he learned from playing off the Texas hardpan. In total he had 31 wins on tour, including three Masters victories. He also played on three winning Ryder Cup teams. His class was best seen when in 1964, and in semi-retirement, he was good enough to tie Tommy Jacobs for the Palm Springs Classic. He lost the play-off.

With his colorful personality, Demaret was a natural for television and for many years (after he succeeded Gene Sarazen), he hosted Shell's *Wonderful World of Golf.* With Jackie Burke, Jr., he co-founded the Champion's Club in Houston, which would host the Ryder Cup and the U.S. Open. He was inducted into the World Golf Hall of Fame in 1983 and died later that year.

Leo Diegel (April 27, 1899–May 8, 1951)

Leo Diegel was one of the most colorful professionals in the interwar period. He was born in Detroit and was good enough to win the city's caddie tournament at age 13. He turned pro three years later. His best years were in the 1920s but he remained a multiple winner in the following decade. In total, he won 30 titles, including two PGA Championships. He also had numerous near misses in the U.S. and British Opens and was a Ryder Cup player on four occasions.

A bad car accident in 1938 more or less ended Diegel's tournament career, but he remained in demand as a club professional and was known as one of the game's great theorists. He wrote a book called *The Nine Bad Shots of Golf,* and Hollywood mogul Joe Schenck once hired him for a full year as his private professional. One of the club posts he held was in Arizona, where he was instrumental in establishing the Tucson Open. Also, toward the end of the war, he became very involved in supporting the Valley Forge project in Philadelphia for returning veterans. It saw a nine-hole course established on hospital grounds exclusively for the use of those who had suffered in combat both mentally and physically. Leo Diegel died from cancer in 1951 at the early age of 52. He was elected into the PGA Hall of Fame in 1955 and into the World Golf Hall of Fame in 2003.

Leonard Dodson (March 29, 1912–January 17, 1997)

Leonard Dodson was one of the many fine golfers to come from the Ozarks (southwest Missouri), who included names such as Horton Smith, Ky Laffoon, and Payne Stewart. Initially he was taught the game by Smith and went on to have a fine career, with eight tournament victories to his name. He was a renowned iron player.

However, it was as a gambler that he achieved his greatest fame. Tales of his hustling are legendary. Sam Snead, no novice himself when it came to gambling, referred to Dodson as the meanest operator he ever saw when the chips were on the table. He would bet on anything, and the newspapers referred to him as golf's "Dizzy Dean" in reference to the baseball player who was famous for his antics. Leonard Dodson died at age 84 and was posthumously inducted into the Ozarks Hall of Fame in 2004.

Ed Dudley (February 19, 1901–October 25, 1963)

"Big" Ed Dudley, at 6 feet 4 inches, was one of the tallest players on tour. He was born in Brunswick, Georgia, and in the early stages of his golfing life benefited from the instruction of Stewart Maiden, the professional at East Lake and renowned teacher of Bobby Jones. Dudley had 15 wins on tour as well as 19 top 10 finishes in the majors. He also played on three Ryder Cup teams. Furthermore, he was appointed as honorary captain for the 1949 matches at Ganton, England. Ben Hogan was the official captain of the successful U.S. team and was friendly with Dudley, who wrote the foreword for Hogan's first instruction book, *Power Golf.*

Dudley had a number of club jobs but he is most associated with the Augusta National Club, where he was head professional from 1932 to 1957 apart from a two-year break (1943–1945, when the course was closed due to the war), and the Broadmoor Club in Colorado, where he taught between 1941 and 1963. He spent the summers in Broadmoor and the winters in Augusta, where one of his pupils was President Dwight Eisenhower. He was also very much involved in tour politics and was PGA President from 1942 to 1948. After he left Augusta, Dudley became attached to the Dorado Beach Club in Puerto Rico; he combined this post with his summer duties at the Broadmoor Club. He remained with the Dorado Beach Club until 1960. During his time there he gave a young Chi Chi Rodriguez his start in professional golf, when he appointed him to be his assistant. Ed Dudley died in Colorado in 1963 and was inducted into the PGA Hall of Fame in 1964.

Olin Dutra (January 17, 1901–May 5, 1983)

Olin Dutra was a Latin American who followed Gene Sarazen's example and made the grade in professional golf. Dutra hailed from California and was of Spanish ancestry. He was also a member of the "golfing brothers" fraternity, which was prevalent in America at the time, such as the Seven Turnesas and Ray and Lloyd Mangrum. Dutra's brother, Mortie, also played the circuit with some distinction. During his illustrious career, Dutra won 19 tour events as well as two majors, the 1932 PGA title and the 1934 U.S. Open. He was also a Ryder Cup player in 1933 and 1935.

Dutra spent most of the Depression era as head pro at the Wilshire Country Club in California. During this period, he won the California PGA title six times. He left Wilshire in 1945 and spent some years trying to advance the game in Mexico. He was inducted into the PGA Hall of Fame in 1962 and died in Newman, California, in 1983, after a long illness.

Al Espinosa (March 24, 1891–January 4, 1957)

Al Espinosa was born in Monterey, California, and came from a large golfing family. Although his best years belonged to the 1920s, he remained competitive during the Depression era and gained four tournament wins. In total, he achieved nine tournament successes as well as finishing as runner-up in both the PGA Championship (1928) and the U.S. Open (1929). Espinosa was also a member of three Ryder Cup teams. As was the norm for this period, he was a club as well as a tournament professional and spent some years in the early 1920s at the Inglewood Club in Seattle.

In the 1930s, Espinosa divided his club career between the Portage Club in Akron during the summer and the Mexico City Country Club in the winter. In 1944, he made his move to Mexico a permanent one; during this period, he won four Mexican Open titles in a row. With his Mexican ancestry and his fluency in Spanish, this move clearly suited him well. Al Espinosa died in 1957 at the age of 65.

Johnny Farrell (April 1, 1901–June 14, 1988)

Johnny Farrell was born in White Plains, New York. Both his parents were Irish. Like other top players such as Manero and Sarazen, Farrell came into the game by caddying in Westchester County. His brother

Jimmy also caddied; as a professional, he worked with Johnny at both Quaker Ridge and St. Augustine, Florida. Farrell was regarded as a fine stylist and was also known for his sartorial elegance. He achieved 22 tournament wins, including the 1928 U.S. Open, and had a number of other top three finishes in the majors. He also played on three Ryder Cup teams. He remained competitive during the Depression era and had some victories, but when he was offered the prestigious club post at Baltusrol, Farrell cut back on his tour appearances, reasoning that supporting a wife and five children demanded a more secure lifestyle than the circuit might offer.

He would remain at Baltusrol until 1972 and became an honorary member of the club. During his time there he achieved a great reputation as a teacher and included Edward, Duke of Windsor, among his pupils. He also taught President Richard Nixon. In 1966, the Farrell family was given the "Golfing Family of the Year" award. (His three sons were all fine players.) Farrell himself was also inducted into the PGA Hall of Fame in 1953. Johnny Farrell died in Florida in 1988, aged 87.

Vic Ghezzi (October 19, 1910–May 30, 1976)

Vic Ghezzi hailed from New Jersey and built up a formidable career both during and after the Depression era. He had 11 wins on tour, including the PGA Championship in 1941, when he defeated Byron Nelson in the final. Like Jimmy Hines and others, he was selected for the 1939 Ryder Cup team but the matches were canceled. Later, in 1946, Ghezzi tied Lloyd Mangrum and Byron Nelson for the U.S. Open title. Mangrum won the play-off.

For a tall man, Ghezzi was not a particularly long hitter but he was a superb short iron player. In addition to his tour success, Ghezzi won five titles in his native New Jersey, three state opens, and two PGA titles. He was also elected to the New Jersey PGA Hall of Fame. Vic Ghezzi died in Florida after a long illness, aged 65.

John Golden (April 2, 1896–January 27, 1936)

John Golden was a New Yorker who learned his trade first as assistant professional at the Tuxedo Club in his home state, and later as head pro. He won nine times on tour and on three occasions was a semi-finalist in the PGA Championship. In addition to these honors, he played on two Ryder Cup teams, where he achieved a perfect record: played three, won three.

The later years of his very short life were spent as head professional at the prestigious Wee Burn Club in Connecticut. On four consecutive occasions (1932–1935) he won the Connecticut Open title. In recognition of his achievements in his adopted state, he was inducted into the Connecticut Golf Hall of Fame in 2000. John Golden died from pneumonia in 1936, age 39. After his premature death, an annual John Golden Memorial tournament was held and contested for by the leading professionals and amateurs from Connecticut, New York and New Jersey.

Ralph Guldahl (November 22, 1911–June 11, 1987)

Ralph Guldahl was a tall Texan. In 1931, at age 19, he became one of the youngest ever winners on tour. However, in the mid–1930s he appeared to lose interest in the game and quit the circuit. Shortly after this, he decided to return. With little income, he required some financial help from Wilson Sporting Goods. This proved to be a great decision, as he went on to dominate the game by winning successive U.S. Opens in 1937 and 1938 and the Masters in 1939. Guldahl also won the highly prestigious Western Open in 1936, 1937 and 1938. His tournament victories totaled 16, all of which were won during the Depression era. He also played in the Ryder Cup of 1937.

By the early 1940s, Guldahl had lost his game, and his disappearance from the winner's circle is one of the great unsolved mysteries of American golf. Some unsuccessful comebacks were attempted before he finally gave up tournament golf entirely. In 1959, Guldahl became a teaching professional at the Braemar Country Club in Tarzana, California, where he was later appointed Golf Professional Emeritus. He was inducted into the World Golf Hall of Fame in 1981 and died peacefully in 1987.

Walter Hagen (December 21, 1892–October 6, 1969)

If Bob Harlow was seen as the father of the tour, then Walter Hagen was undoubtedly the father of American professionals. Moreover, even if his best years were behind him during the Depression era, he remained a formidable player and a great attraction for sponsors and fans alike. Hagen was born in Rochester, New York, and learned his golf as a caddie. His record bears comparison with the best in the history of the game. He had 45 wins on tour, including 11 major titles and 30 "other" victories including the French Open title of 1920. Seven of his tour wins came during the 1930s.

In addition to these honors, Hagen captained the first six U.S. Ryder Cup teams and played in five of these competitions. He died in Michigan in 1969. As a mark of his considerable contribution to professional golf,

Arnold Palmer was among the pallbearers at his funeral. Hagen was posthumously inducted into the World Golf Hall of Fame in 1974.

Bob Harlow (October 21, 1899–November 15, 1954)

Bob Harlow is generally regarded as the "father" of the tour. Originally a journalist, he was always interested in the theater and, indeed, married a singer. These theatrical qualities would serve him well both as Walter Hagen's manager and as tournament director, as he always believed that golfers had to put on a show. It was this ability to know what both sponsors and the public wanted which helped Harlow advance the professional game during the Depression era. He was also a golfing globalist who saw the potential for developing the game well beyond the shores of America.

After his time as tournament director, Harlow went back to writing on golf. In 1947 he founded *Golf World* magazine. He died at age 55 in Pinehurst, which had become his adopted home, and was posthumously inducted into the World Golf Hall of Fame in 1988.

E.J. "Dutch" Harrison (March 29, 1910–June 19, 1982)

Many golfers from this era had nicknames, but Harrison was unusual in that he had two: "Dutch" and "The Arkansas Traveler." "Dutch" Harrison hailed from Arkansas and was born into a poor, sharecropping family. He followed the usual route into the game by caddying and turned pro in 1930. While his best years came after the Depression era, there is no doubt that he learned the professional game in the 1930s, achieving his initial victories on tour with two wins in 1939. During this decade he supplemented his income with his ability to "hustle" and played in many big money matches.

Harrison would go on to win a total of 18 events and played in three successful Ryder Cup teams. He was undefeated in his singles matches. Harrison was also good enough to win the Vardon Trophy for best scoring average in 1954. He was elected to the PGA Hall of Fame in 1962. In later years he would become head professional at the Forest Hills Club in St. Louis, where he remained until 1975. He died from heart failure in 1982, aged 72.

Jimmy Hines (December 29, 1903–May 11, 1986)

Along with Jimmy Thomson and Craig Wood, Jimmy Hines was one of the game's big hitters during this era. He was born in New York and learned the game as a caddie on Long Island. In total, he achieved nine victories on tour and was good enough to earn selection for the 1939 Ryder Cup team. Unfortunately, however, the matches were canceled due to the outbreak of war.

Apart from his tournament career, Hines was both a club professional and a course designer. Among his creations was the Avondale course in Palm Desert, California. He is also credited with being among the first to develop the electric golf cart. He died in California in 1986.

Ben Hogan (August 13, 1912–July 25, 1997)

In any discussion of "all-time greats" in golf, Ben Hogan is invariably either at or near the very top. While his best years came after the Great Depression, this was the era in which he learned the professional game and achieved his first successes. Hogan was born in Texas into a poor background and was introduced to golf when caddying at the Glen Garden Club. It is part of golfing folklore that another caddie there was Byron Nelson. After many disappointments, Hogan finally broke through with his first win in 1940; he followed this with four more tour victories the next year. After this initial breakthrough, his career included 64 tour wins, with nine victories in the majors. He is one of only five golfers to complete the Grand Slam of golf. The others are Gene Sarazen, Jack Nicklaus, Gary Player and Tiger Woods.

Apart from these successes, Hogan gained fame as being the first golfer to have a movie made of his life. This was *Follow the Sun,* starring Glen Ford as Hogan, and it charted his incredible recovery from a motor vehicle accident in 1949. He also wrote (along with Herbert Warren Wind) golf's most famous instruction book, *Five Lessons.* In 1953, he founded the Hogan golf equipment company, which he ran until 1960, when it was sold. He remained on the board of the company for many years after this. Ben Hogan died in 1997 at Fort Worth, Texas.

Jules Huot (January 7, 1908–February 2, 1999)

Jules Huot was born in Quebec and at an early age started caddying at the Royal Quebec club. His proficiency here led to him becoming assistant professional. Throughout his life he combined club duties with tournament golf both in his native Canada and south of the border in the United States. In 1937 he made history by becoming the first Canadian to win a U.S. tour event when he captured the General Brock Open from a field which included Byron Nelson, Ben Hogan and the big-hitting Jimmy Thomson.

Although Huot played in many events on tour, much of his time was spent in Canada. Here he won many domestic titles, including the Canadian PGA on three occasions. He also represented Canada in the Canada Cup in 1954. Huot came from a golfing family and three of his brothers became professionals. The last 25 years of his golfing career were spent as head professional at the Laval sur le Lac club. He was inducted into the Canadian Golf Hall of Fame in 1977 and died at age 91.

Ky Laffoon (December 23, 1908–March 17, 1984)

Ky Laffoon was undoubtedly one of the most colorful personalities to play the tour in the 1930s. He was born in Arkansas and, because of his swarthy features, was often thought to have Native American blood. In fact, he was of French/English/Irish origin. Nevertheless, Laffoon did not discourage the media from pursuing the Native American angle, as he felt it added color to his profile. Indeed, he often answered to the name "Chief." His best year on tour was 1934, when he recorded four wins. In total he achieved 10 victories on tour and was good enough to make the all-star American Ryder Cup team of 1935. Laffoon also had a number of fine finishes in the majors, notably a third place in the 1936 U.S. Open and a semi-final spot in the 1937 PGA Championship.

However, despite this undoubted talent, golfing history seems to have recognized his bizarre and often outrageous behavior more than his achievements. Many stories have been attributed to him, some apocryphal and some not. For example, one tale suggested that he punished his putter by tying it to the boot of his car so that by the time he reached the next tour stop the putter would have learned how to behave. According to Ky, however, it was a sand wedge and he was merely trying to sharpen the leading edge of the club. Regardless of which version is correct, he was undoubtedly a volatile character but one with a wonderful swing and a deep knowledge of the game. After a long battle with cancer, he took his own life in Springfield, Missouri, in 1984. He was inducted into the Ozarks Hall of Fame in 2009.

Lawson Little (June 23, 1910–February 1, 1968)

Lawson Little was born in Rhode Island but spent most his life in California. Outside of Bobby Jones, Little had perhaps the best amateur record of any American player. He was a Walker Cup player and won the U.S. and British Amateur titles in two consecutive years, 1934 and 1935. His professional career was not as glittering as his amateur experience, but he recorded eight tour wins, including the 1940 U.S. Open.

Little was famous for his long hitting but also possessed a wonderful short game. The years after World War II were not always kind to him, especially regarding his health, but he did play in the occasional tournament, notably the Crosby pro-am. He died at the young age of 57 at his home overlooking Pebble Beach. He was inducted into the World Golf Hall of Fame in 1980.

Willie MacFarlane (June 29, 1890–August 15, 1961)

Willie MacFarlane from Aberdeen, Scotland, came to America a little later than some of the other Scots who made such a mark on the game in their adopted land. However, he, too, was destined to make a significant impact, notably when defeating Bobby Jones to win the 1925 U.S. Open title. Tall and gentlemanly in his bearing, MacFarlane was known as an expert shot-maker rather than a "big hitter." He won 21 times on tour and even if his greatest moment was in the 1920s, he had numerous victories during the Depression era.

MacFarlane had a long association with the Oak Ridge Club in Tuckahoe, New York. During the 1920s he also spent time teaching at the Hollywood Club in Florida. After the war, he taught at the Miami Shores Club. In the later years of his life he ran a driving range. Willie MacFarlane died from a heart attack in Florida in 1961, aged 71.

Tony Manero (April 4, 1905–October 22, 1989)

Tony Manero was one of the many Italian Americans to emerge in professional golf during this era. Like his friend Gene Sarazen, whose original name was Saraceni, he changed his name, from Mainiero to Manero. He was also similar to Sarazen in that he started out as a caddy in New York State. Manero was the possessor of a fine singing voice and at one time, he toyed with the idea of becoming a professional crooner. However, he committed to a career in golf. In total he won eight tournaments, including the 1936 U.S. Open at Baltusrol. He was also a member of the successful 1937 U.S. Ryder Cup team.

In the postwar era, Manero stepped back from golf and devoted much of his time to Manero's Restaurant in Greenwich, Connecticut, where he was a popular host for many years. Indeed, when the tour stopped at nearby Westchester, the restaurant was a regular venue for many of the game's leading players. However, Manero did play occasionally, and his game was good enough to win the local Westchester Open in 1948. In 1964 he was inducted into the Connecticut Golf Hall of Fame. A similar award followed in 1976, this time from the Metropolitan PGA Hall of Fame. Tony Manero died of heart failure in Greenwich, aged 84.

Ray Mangrum (June 17, 1910–April 2, 1975)

Ray Mangrum was the older brother of Lloyd Mangrum and another of the "Texas Rangers" who made an impact during this period. He spent time at the Cliff Dale Country Club before moving on to a position at the prestigious Oakmont club. During his time there, he twice won the Pennsylvania State Championship. It was also at Oakmont, in 1935, that he met his future bride, who came to watch him play in a tournament. The meeting was reported to be "love at first sight" but the marriage ended in divorce. Interestingly, while on honeymoon, Mangrum finished fourth at the U.S. Open, which was played at Oakmont that year.

In total he won five tour events, one of which was a play-off victory over Ben Hogan in Pensacola in 1946. This was the period when Hogan and Nelson dominated the tour, and this victory showed the class of Ray Mangrum. He died in 1975.

Harold "Jug" McSpaden (July 21, 1908–April 22, 1996)

"Jug" McSpaden came from Kansas and learned the game by caddying at the Mission Hills Club in Kansas City. He turned professional in 1926 and his promise was recognized by Horton Smith, who invited him to go to California to play some tournaments. McSpaden did not feel he was ready and declined the offer. This was probably a wise decision, as in the early years of his career he was a long but erratic hitter. However, after receiving some advice from Walter Hagen and McDonald Smith, he changed his approach and became a more methodical player, much like Horton Smith. In total, McSpaden won 17 times on tour but is often remembered for the number of near misses he had during Byron Nelson's streak of 1945. In fact, McSpaden helped start Nelson's "12 in a row" run by partnering him to victory in the Miami Fourball. He was selected for the 1939 Ryder Cup team, but its competition was canceled due to war.

In the years after the war, McSpaden played less and became involved in the golf clothing business. However, he also became a course architect and designed the Dub's Dread course in Kansas. This was (at the time, certainly) the longest course in America at over 8,000 yards. To promote the venue, an exhibition match was held in 1968 between McSpaden and Nelson and Nicklaus and Palmer. The "young pros" gave the veterans 50 yards off the tee on each hole and won the match one up. McSpaden is a member of the PGA Hall of Fame and in 1991, was elected to the Kansas Golf Hall of Fame. In 1996, he and his wife died from accidental carbon monoxide poisoning.

Dick Metz (May 29, 1908–May 5, 1993)

"Handsome" Dick Metz came from Arkansas City and joined the tour in 1930. In total he won 10 official tour events. He was a renowned master of the long irons. Apart from his celebrated marriage to movie star Jean Chatburn, Metz was colorful in other ways. Possessed of a fiery temperament, Metz had a few disagreements with the tour and on one occasion is alleged to have punched tour boss Fred Corcoran. This event took place at a tournament in Del Monte, California, and Corcoran said that Metz hit him without even "shouting fore."

From the mid–1950s on, Metz devoted most of his time to cattle ranching in a number of states. However, his class as a golfer remained; he was good enough to win the U.S. Senior PGA title in 1960, as well as the World Senior Championship. His final cattle ranch was near his birthplace in Arkansas City, Kansas, and he died there in 1993 of a self-inflicted gunshot wound.

Fred Morrison (1900–1959)

Along with the Dutras and the Espinosas, the Morrisons were another famous golfing family to emerge from California during the early decades of the 20th century. Fred was the most prominent player but his brother, Alex, gained fame as an instructor and wrote a best-selling book, *A New Way to Better Golf*. Alex is often seen as being one of the fathers of modern golf teaching, with his use of cameras being very advanced for that era. Another brother, Bob, also made teaching golf his career.

Apart from playing, Fred Morrison also taught; for many years he was attached to the exclusive Midwick Club in Los Angeles. Among his students there was Hollywood icon Douglas Fairbanks, Sr. Morrison had many local triumphs, such as his four victories in the Southern Californian Open. However, it was his victory in the 1932 Agua Caliente Open and its first prize of $5,000 which saw him rise to national fame. His fame did not last long, and some bad financial decisions and poor health saw him more or less retire from the tour at the end of the 1930s. He returned to teaching and died at the relatively young age of 59.

Byron Nelson (February 4, 1912–September 26, 2006)

John Byron Nelson was born in Ellis County, Texas, in the same year as his long-time rivals, Sam Snead and Ben Hogan. He graduated from the caddie yard at the Glen Garden Club to the professional ranks in 1932. As well as forming the usual (for that period) attachments to prominent clubs such as Ridgewood and Inverness, he made a massive impact on tour during the 1930s, which laid the ground for his ascent into "legend" status during the 1940s. He was known as one of the game's greatest ever ball strikers, and for some he is seen as the "father" of the modern golf swing. In total he won 52 tour events, including five majors, and played on two Ryder Cup teams.

After 1945 and a record 11 wins in a row (he won a fourball with "Jug" McSpaden before the first of these victories), Nelson's interest in the tour appeared to wane. As he now had financial security, he fulfilled his life's ambition and bought a farm near Dallas. Appropriately this was called "the Fairway Ranch." In semi-retirement he was still good enough to win the French Open in 1955, and he captained the U.S. Ryder Cup team in 1965. He also enjoyed success as a television commentator and mentored top players Ken Venturi and Tom Watson. The Byron Nelson Classic (which he hosted up to his death) remains one the tour's most prestigious tournaments. During his career Nelson received numerous awards, such as the PGA Lifetime Achievement Award in 1997. Shortly after his death in 2006, he posthumously received the Congressional Gold Medal.

Ed "Porky" Oliver (September 6, 1916–September 21, 1961)

Ed Oliver was born in Wilmington, Delaware, in 1916 and gained national prominence at the end of the Depression era, when he won three times in 1940. In total he achieved eight victories on tour and played on three successful Ryder Cup teams in 1947, 1951 and 1953. It was, perhaps, for his "nearly man" tag, however, that he is best remembered, apart from being disqualified from the 1940 U.S. Open when he had posted a score which would have tied Lawson Little and Gene Sarazen. He also finished second in the same championship in 1952. Furthermore, he was a beaten finalist in the PGA Championship of 1946 when Ben Hogan was the winner, and the same player beat Oliver (who finished in second place) in the 1953 Masters.

Oliver continued to play successfully into the late 1950s. He won the Houston Open in 1958 and the Jamaican Open a year later. However, in 1960 he was diagnosed with cancer, to which he responded by fighting to raise awareness of the disease. In total his efforts saw $20,000 raised for cancer research. In recognition of his contribution to professional golf, he was appointed honorary captain of the 1961 Ryder Cup team. The matches that year were held in Royal Lytham and St. Anne's but Oliver did not make the trip. He died in September 1961 at age 45. The

Ed Oliver public course in his hometown of Wilmington bears his name to this day.

Sam Parks, Jr. (June 23, 1909–August 7, 1997)

Sam Parks, Jr., was born in Bellevue, Pennsylvania. He was unusual for a golf professional of that era, in that he learned the game in the exclusive Highland Country Club in Pittsburgh, rather than the caddie yard. He also went to Pittsburgh University. As an amateur he was very successful in local events. He had no plans to turn pro, at least until the economic collapse of the early 1930s changed everything. Parks had planned to follow his father into the insurance business or some area of the financial services but with no work available, he became a professional golfer in 1932. His first job was in Uniontown, Pennsylvania. Parks's place in golfing history came about because of his surprise win in the 1935 U.S. Open at Oakmont. It was his only official victory, although he did win some local tournaments such as the Pennsylvania Open. He also made the Ryder Cup team in 1935.

His career as a professional, however, did not last long. Eventually Parks took a job with U.S. Steel during the mid–1940s; he worked there as a successful salesman for roughly 30 years—so he did have his business career after all. Sam Parks, Jr., died in Clearwater, Florida, in 1997, aged 88.

Toney Penna (January 15, 1905–August 6, 1995)

Toney Penna was unusual among the band of Italian American professionals in that he was actually born in Italy, in Naples. His family emigrated to America when he was young, and he grew up and caddied in Harrison, New York, in the same neighborhood as Gene Sarazen. Penna won four times on tour but had many other fine finishes, such as being third behind Ralph Guldahl at the 1938 U.S. Open.

Arguably, it was as a teacher and club designer that Penna gained even greater fame. Many of his teaching skills were learned when working with Tommy Armour at Boca Raton during the 1930s. He was a longtime salesman for the MacGregor equipment company. Apart from Ben Hogan, other players he signed up for MacGregor included Jimmy Demaret and Jug McSpaden. His true *forte* was in club design, however, and after years with MacGregor, he later started his own firm, the Toney Penna Golf Company. Many of his designs were sought after and used by leading players. Penna was also friends with many celebrities from the 1950s and 1960s. Among these was Perry Como, who became a director in Penna's golf company. Another was Bing Crosby: Penna coached Bing's son,

Nathaniel, to victory in the 1981 U.S. Amateur Championship at Pebble Beach. The younger Crosby later became president of Toney Penna Golf. Toney Penna died in Palm Beach Gardens, Florida, in 1995, aged 90.

Henry Picard (November 28, 1906–April 30, 1997)

Henry Picard was born in Plymouth. Like many of his fellow professionals, his entry into golf was as a caddie—in Picard's case, at the local Plymouth Country Club. Here he showed promise as a player and was recommended to the Charleston Club in South Carolina by the club professional at Plymouth, Donald Vinton. He remained at Plymouth as both assistant and club professional from 1925 until 1935, when he went to the Hershey Club in Pennsylvania. It was the members at Charleston who raised $150 to send Picard on tour. This was a significant gesture at a time when many clubs (including Charleston) were in financial difficulty. Picard always credited instructor Alex Morrison (Fred's brother) with helping him to develop his swing, which was regarded as one of golf's finest. In total he won 26 times on tour, including the Masters and the PGA Championship. He was also a Ryder Cup player in 1935 and 1937.

Apart from his club attachments at Charleston and Hershey, Picard spent time at a number of other clubs, including the prestigious Seminole, Florida, and Twin Hills, Oklahoma, clubs. He was regarded as one the game's finest teachers and counted among his pupils Beth Daniel, who won 33 times on the LPGA tour. Henry Picard died, aged 90, in Charleston, the place of his first professional job. He was inducted into the World Golf Hall of Fame in 2006.

Johnny Revolta (April 5, 1911–March 3, 1991)

Johnny Revolta was born in St. Louis. As well as starting the game as a caddie, he began playing with home-made clubs. When he became a professional, he held a number of club posts before landing the prestigious job at the Evanston Club in Skokie, Illinois. He would remain there as head professional until 1966. Nineteen thirty-five was a big year for Revolta: he finished as the leading money winner that year as well as collecting his only major title, the PGA Championship. In total he won 18 times on tour and played in the Ryder Cup in 1935 and 1937.

Not one of the game's long hitters, Revolta's prowess was in the short game. In 1949, he released a book called *Short Cuts to Better Golf.* The book became a best seller and remains available to this day. After retiring from the tour in the early 1950s, Revolta was much in demand as a teacher both at Evanston and at the Mission Hills Club, Rancho Mirage, California. In fact, after his official retirement in 1966, he continued to teach at Evanston until a few years before his death. He also received numerous honors, such as being elected to the PGA Hall of Fame in 1963 and the Illinois PGA Hall of Fame in 1989. He died in Palm Springs, California, in 1991, aged 79.

Paul Runyan (July 12, 1908–March 17, 2002)

Paul Runyan from Hot Springs, Arkansas, was one of the smallest professionals of this era, yet undoubtedly one of the most successful. After graduating as a caddie at Hot Springs, he spent some years at the local Concordia Club, where he later claimed he honed his game. In 1931, he joined Craig Wood as his assistant at the Forest Hills Club in New Jersey, before moving to the Metropolis Club in White Plains, New York. This was the springboard for his graduation to the tour for the 1931–1932 season, as the members at Metropolis gave him financial backing for the season. In total Runyan won 29 times on tour; between the years of 1933 and 1934, he won a remarkable 16 events. Included in his 29 victories were two PGA Championships and four top 4 finishes in the Masters. He also played in the 1933 and 1935 Ryder Cup matches.

Runyan was known as an excellent teacher and one of his books, *The Short Way to Lower Scoring*, was seen as a very influential book on the short game. However, as well as teaching, he remained competitive in his senior years, winning the PGA Senior title in both 1961 and 1962. He also received a host of honors, such as his induction into the World Golf Hall of Fame in 1990. He was inducted into the World Golf Teachers Hall of Fame as well. Even in his final years his enthusiasm for the game never waned: at age 91, he took part in the annual par–3 tournament at the 2000 Masters. He died in Palm Springs, California, in 2002.

Gene Sarazen (February 27, 1902–May 10, 1999)

Gene Sarazen was the first of the Italian American professionals to make a major impact on the game of golf. The son of an Italian carpenter, Sarazen was introduced to golf while caddying at the Apawamis Club in Rye, New York. Another caddie there at that time was future television personality, Ed Sullivan. When Sarazen turned pro, his first job as head professional was at the Titusville club in Pennsylvania. He was 19 years old. He had a number of club jobs subsequently but also spent a great deal of time (especially in the 1930s) touring the world with Joe Kirkwood or Walter Hagen. In these harsh times, this was a more secure form of income. However, it was as a tournament player that Sarazen is best remembered, and his records stand comparison with those of the game's greats. He was the first to win the Grand Slam of golf; he had 39 tour wins, including seven majors; and he played on six Ryder Cup teams. He also had golfing longevity, winning his first U.S. Open in 1922 and losing to Lawson Little for the same prize in 1940.

Apart from his tournament prowess, Sarazen made other contributions to golf. He is credited with inventing the modern sand wedge and for many years was a popular host on Shell's *Wonderful World of Golf;* the show which helped bring golf to a global audience during the 1950s and 1960s. But he still played the game effectively—indeed, in both 1954 and 1958, Sarazen won the U.S. Senior PGA title. He was also a farmer in both New York State and Connecticut, which earned him the nickname "the Squire." He was elected into the World Golf Hall of Fame in 1974 and he died in Florida in 1999, aged 97.

Herman Densmore "Denny" Shute (October 25, 1904– May 13, 1974)

Denny Shute was literally born into golf, as his father, Herman, was a British professional who emigrated to America. The Ohio-born Shute quickly learned the game and turned professional in 1928. During the 1930s, the quietly spoken Shute would become one of the best players in the world as well as one of the game's finest stylists. He won 16 times on tour, a list of victories that included two successive PGA titles in 1936 and 1937. He was on three Ryder Cup teams: 1931, 1933 and 1937. Arguably, his greatest achievement was when he won the British Open in St. Andrews in 1933, making him one of a select group of Americans to win the title at the "Home of Golf." In winning, he beat Craig Wood by five shots in a 36-hole play-off.

Shute's tour career began to taper off during the war years. In 1945 he became head professional at the Portage Club in Akron, Ohio. Here he succeeded Al Espinosa. He would stay at Portage for the rest of his professional career, until 1972. He remained a formidable player, however, and in 1950 won the 72-hole Ohio Open Championship, a tournament he had already won on three consecutive occasions from 1929 to 1931. Shute was elected to the PGA Hall of Fame in 1957 and (posthumously) to the World Golf Hall of Fame in 2008. He died in Akron in 1974, aged 69.

Horton Smith (May 22, 1908–October 15, 1963)

Horton Smith was born in Springfield, Missouri, and learned his golf at the local Springfield Club, where his father was a member. He was fortunate that the professional there at the time, Neil Crose, took a keen interest in his game and helped the young Smith develop his prodigious talent. The two men remained firm friends. Smith turned pro in 1926, and his elegant swing and superb putting touch saw him win 32 tour titles. Included in these was a win in the first ever Masters in 1934—a feat he repeated two years later. He also played on five Ryder Cup teams.

Smith was known as a quiet and intellectual professional but he made numerous headlines in 1938, when he married the Singer Sewing Machine heiress, Barbara Bourne. The marriage ended in divorce in 1945. On his discharge from the Army Air Corps after the war, Smith became head professional at the Detroit Club, Michigan. During this period he also served as president of the PGA, from 1952 to 1954. In 1962, Smith won the Bobby Jones Award for sportsmanship. In 1990, he was posthumously inducted into the World Golf Hall of Fame. In later life, he suffered from Hodgkin's disease and while watching the Ryder Cup matches in Atlanta in the autumn of 1963, he collapsed. He was brought back to Detroit, where he died on October 15. The Horton Smith Municipal course in Springfield bears testimony to the enormous contribution he made to golf both as a player and as an administrator.

MacDonald Smith (March 8, 1892–August 31, 1949)

MacDonald Smith was one of the many immigrant Scottish professionals who came to America at the turn of the 20th century. Born in Carnoustie, he caddied on the famous Scottish links as a boy and later followed the path of his four golfing brothers, all of whom enjoyed successful professional careers in America. In fact, as the youngest in the family, Smith traveled with his parents, who also decided to emigrate. He held a number of club posts, such as that of teaching professional at the famed Oakmont Club in Pennsylvania. During his time there he won the Pennsylvania State Open in 1914. After serving in World War I, he moved to the West Coast. After periods at other clubs, including the Olympic in San Francisco, he settled at the Oakmont Country Club in California in 1934. He remained there as head professional until 1946.

Smith, however, was best known as a tournament player and as one of the game's great stylists. In total, he won 24 tour events and had many near misses in the majors. Many named him the greatest player never to win a major championship. He died in California in 1949, aged 57.

Sam Snead (May 27, 1912–May 23. 2002)

Sam Snead was born in Virginia and started caddying at his local Homestead Club at age seven. He would later become professional at the nearby Cascades Club, where there was little to be made in terms of money but where he was able to practice and develop what is generally regarded as the most graceful swing the game has ever known. "I beat sod" was how Snead described the amount of practice he did at Cascades. He came on tour in the mid–1930s. His win at the 1937 Oakland Open was the first of 82 official tour victories. Included in these were seven major titles, but famously he failed to win the U.S. Open. Snead also played on seven Ryder Cup teams and was captain on three occasions.

His longevity in the professional game was extraordinary. In 1974, aged 62, he finished third, three shots behind Lee Trevino, in the PGA Championship. And at the age of 67, he shot 66 in the 1979 Quad Cities Open. He also won 14 Senior titles between 1964 and 1982 and is generally credited with being instrumental in establishing the lucrative "over 50s" circuit, which is now known as the Champions Tour. The game bestowed numerous honors on Snead, including induction into the World Golf Hall of Fame in 1974 and the PGA Lifetime Achievement Award in 1998. He died from a stroke in Hot Springs, Virginia, in 2002, just four days short of his 90th birthday.

Jimmy Thomson (October 29, 1908–June 28, 1985)

Jimmy Thomson from North Berwick was one of the major attractions in golf during the Depression era. His father Wilfred was also a pro who took up a club job in Virginia in 1921. Jimmy, his mother and his sister followed Wilfred a year after he took up his post. From the start, Thomson was a long hitter and claimed that much of this prowess came from practicing hitting balls with his feet together. During his career, Thomson was attached to a number of clubs, such as the Broadmoor Country Club in Colorado. Another was the Lakewood Country Club in California, where he met silent screen star, Viola Dana. The couple were married in 1930 but the marriage ended in divorce in 1945.

Thomson's tournament record shows only two tour wins in America, but he came close in the majors—notably in 1935, when he bogeyed the last four holes to lose by just two shots to Sam Parks at Oakmont. He was also runner-up to Denny Shute in the 1936 PGA Championship. Overall, his contribution to golf during this period was significant, as he was a big "box office" draw because of his powerful hitting. He won many long driving competitions, which were very popular at the time. He was also part of the "Spalding Fourball" which did so much to popularize the game during the 1930s. Thomson served in the U.S. Coast Guard during the war, and later he appeared in some movies with a golfing theme, including one with Bing Crosby called *Swing with Bing*. He also worked as promotional director for the Dunlop equipment company for a number of years. He died in Miami in 1985, aged 76.

Joe Turnesa (January 31, 1901–July 15, 1991)

Joe Turnesa was the third among seven golfing brothers who grew up in New York County. His father, who hailed from Italy, became green-keeper at the Fairview Club, which paved the way for Joe and his brothers to become caddies and learn the game. Joe was undoubtedly the best player in the family; he went on to win 14 tour events as well as play in two Ryder Cup matches. During one Ryder Cup trip, he won the 1929 *Yorkshire Evening News* tournament, as it was common for the U.S. team to play in some event when the matches were played in Britain. Turnesa also finished as runner-up in both the U.S. Open and the PGA Championship.

During his playing career he was attached to a number of clubs, such as the Jungle Club in Florida and the Wampanoag Club in Hartford. However, it was perhaps later in life when he enjoyed his most fulfilling period as a club professional—namely, at the Sara Bay club in Florida, where he taught in the 1970s and 1980s. He was held in such esteem that he was made an honorary member. To this day, a Joe Turnesa Memorial Scholarship tournament is held annually at the club. Turnesa died in Florida in 1991, aged 90.

Craig Wood (November 18, 1901–May 7, 1968)

Along with Jimmy Thomson, Craig Wood was regarded as one of the power hitters of this period. He was also one of the most popular and well-liked professionals on tour. Born in Lake Placid, New York, Wood reportedly developed his strength from working in his father's lumber yard as a boy. He was attached to a number of clubs, such as Deal in the early 1930s, where he took the emerging Dick Metz under his wing. From 1939 to 1945, he was the professional at Winged Foot, the scene of many of golf's majors. Later in life he spent time teaching in the Bahamas. As a tournament player he built up a formidable record, with 21 tour titles including the U.S. Open and the Masters in 1941.

Wood also played on three Ryder Cup teams. He had the "distinction" of losing the British and U.S. Opens, and the Masters in a 36-hole play-off. He was elected to the PGA Hall of Fame in 1956 and to the World Golf Hall of Fame in 2008, 40 years after his death. He died in Palm Beach, Florida, aged 66, but is buried in his hometown of Lake Placid, where the Craig Wood Golf Course still honors his name.

Chapter Notes

Introduction

1. G. Sarazen and H.W. Wind, *Thirty Years of Championship Golf* (London: A. & C. Black, 1950), pp. 123–124.

2. G. Tindall and D. Shi, *America* (London: Norton, 1993), p. 714.

3. *The Sunday Morning Star*, December 27, 1925.

4. *The Toledo News-Bee*, September 8, 1925.

5. Richard J. Moss, *Golf and the American Country Club* (Urbana: University of Illinois Press, 2001), p. 104.

6. *Ibid.*, p. 112.

7. Sarazen and Wind, p. 123.

8. *Ibid.*, p, 124.

9. W. Hagen, *The Walter Hagen Story by The Haig Himself* (New York: Simon & Schuster, 1956), p. 117.

10. *The American Golfer,* December 1926.

11. P. Welch, "A Focus on Women's Sport in Florida During the Depression Decade," *North American Society for Sports History, Proceedings and Newsletter* (1996), pp. 46–47.

12. *The American Golfer*, Vol. 29, 1926.

13. *The Milwaukee Journal*, October 3, 1900.

14. A. Barkow, *Golf's Golden Grind* (New York: Harcourt Brace Jovanovich, 1974), p. 60.

15. *The Providence News*, October 28, 1902.

16. *The New York Times,* January 18, 1916.

17. *Sporting Life*, Vol. 68, 1916.

18. *The American Golfer,* April 1916.

19. *The American Golfer,* May 1928.

20. *Ibid.*

21. *The Schenectady Gazette*, August 5, 1925.

22. Barkow, *Golf's Golden Grind,* p. 88.

23. *The American Golfer*, January 1925.

24. Hagen, p. 119.

25. *The Rochester Evening Journal*, February 20, 1926.

26. *The Miami News*, November 15, 1925.

27. *The St. Petersburg Times*, November 10, 1925.

28. Sarazen and Wind, pp. 116–127.

Chapter 1

1. C. Degler, *Out of Our Past* (New York: Harper Colophon, 1970), p. 379.

2. *Ibid.*, p. 389.

3. Tindall and Shi, p. 734.

4. Degler, p. 390.

5. "The Presidential Papers of Franklin D. Roosevelt," Item 18, January 23, 1937.

6. Letter from Burning Tree Golf Club to FDR, July 12, 1940.

7. *The Palm Beach Post*, October 9, 1935.

8. George B. Kirsch, *Golf in America* (Urbana: University of Illinois Press, 2009), p. 110.

9. *The New York Times*, April 21, 1896.

10. *The American Golfer,* Vol. 24, 1921.

11. *The Milwaukee Sentinel,* November 21, 1913.

12. Moss, p. 114.

13. B.S. Klein, *Discovering Donald Ross* (New York: John Wiley & Sons, 2001), p. 194.

14. *The New York Times,* June 14, 2009.

15. *Golfdom*, May 1936, p. 19.

16. *Golf Digest,* June 2002, p. 159.

17. *Golfdom,* May 1938.

18. *Golfdom,* June 1938.

19. *Golfdom,* October 1936.

20. *Golfdom,* May 1940.

21. *The New York Times,* April 28, 1936.

22. *The New York Times,* June 1936, p. 34.

23. M. Benton, *The Velvet Touch* (Detroit: Ann Arbor Press, 1965), pp. 100–102.

24. *Golfdom,* May 1937, p. 21.

25. *Golfdom,* September 1937.

26. R.J. Moss, *Eden in the Pines* (Southern Pines, NC: Pilot, 2005), p. 82.

27. *Ibid.,* p. 89.

28. H.W. Wind, *The Story of American Golf* (New York: Alfred A. Knopf, 1975), p. 214.

29. Club historian, Salem Country Club.

30. *Ibid.*

31. *Ibid.*

32. Club historian, Inglewood Country Club.

33. *The Chicago Daily Tribune*, April 6, 1932.

34. *Ibid.*

35. T.W. Cronin, *The Spirit of Medinah* (Medinah, IL: Medinah Country Club, 2001), abstract.

36. *The Telegraph Herald,* August 11, 1935.

37. Club historian, Glen Oak Country Club.

38. *The News & Courier*, March 20, 1932.

39. *The Chicago Daily Tribune,* June 6, 1934.

40. R.S. Trebus and R.C. Wolfe, Jr., *Baltusrol: 100 Years* (Lynchburg, VA: Progress Printing, 1995), p. 20.

41. *Ibid.*

42. *The Chicago Daily Tribune,* May 28, 1931.

43. *The Chicago Daily Tribune,* November 8, 1931.

44. *The Pittsburgh Press*, June 1, 1931.

45. *The Pittsburgh Press,* May 1, 1932.

46. *The Prescott Evening Courier*, August 3, 1934.

47. *Golf Illustrated*, November 1932.

48. *Golf Illustrated,* February 1932.

49. *Golf Illustrated,* April 1933.

50. *The Pittsburgh Press,* December 23, 1934.

51. *The Pittsburgh Press,* February 4, 1934.

52. *PGA Magazine*, January 1931.

53. Wind, p. 214.

Chapter 2

1. *Time Magazine,* January 17, 1938.

2. *The Berkley Daily Gazette,* January 20, 1932.

3. *The Tuscaloosa News,* March 23, 1930.

4. *Ibid.*

5. *The Pittsburgh Press,* March 13, 1932.

6. Stephen R. Lowe, *Sir Walter and Mr. Jones* (Chelsea, MI: Sleeping Bear Press, 2000), p. 246.

7. Barkow, *Golf's Golden Grind,* p. 94.

8. *The American Golfer,* April 1932.

9. *The Sydney Morning Herald,* September 7, 1934.

10. *The Miami News,* June 2, 1935.

11. *PGA Magazine,* April 1932.

12. *Ibid.*

13. *The Lewiston Daily Sun,* January 15, 1937.

14. A. Barkow, *The Golden Era of Golf* (New York: Thomas Dunne, 2000), p. 60.

15. *Ibid.*

16. Barkow, *Golf's Golden Grind,* p. 107.

17. Judy Corcoran, *Fred Corcoran: The Man Who Sold Golf* (New York: Gray, 2010), Chapter 2.

18. *The Evening Independent,* August 10, 1939.

19. F. Corcoran, *Unplayable Lies* (New York: Duell, Sloan & Pearce, 1964), p. 60.

20. *Ibid.,* p. 54.

21. *Ibid.,* p. 57.

22. *The Prescott Evening Courier,* April 8, 1937.

23. *The St. Petersburg Times,* April 2, 1938.

24. *PGA Magazine,* May 1939.

Chapter 3

1. Wind, p. 213.

2. *Time,* August 15, 1932.

3. *The Westchester Journal News,* May 16, 1999.

4. James Dodson, *American Triumvirate* (New York: Alfred A. Knopf, 2012), p. 13.

5. *The Tuscaloosa News,* March 6, 1930.

6. See the Introduction.

7. *The American Golfer,* July 1934.

8. *Ibid.*

9. *The Miami News,* March 27, 1927.

10. *The Pittsburgh Press,* March 15, 1928.

11. *The Pittsburgh Press,* January 19, 1931.

12. *PGA Magazine,* February 1931.

13. *Time Magazine,* July 4, 1932.

14. *The Calgary Herald,* October 30, 1931.

15. *The Pittsburgh Press,* July 10, 1931.

16. *The Pittsburgh Press,* June 11, 1931.

17. *The New York Times,* July 6, 1931.

18. *Ibid.*

19. *Time Magazine,* July 20, 1931.

20. *The Leader Post,* July 15, 1931.

21. *The Milwaukee Journal,* June 19, 1931.

22. *The American Golfer,* Vol. 36, 1932.

23. B. Nelson, *How I Played the Game* (New York: Dell, 1993), p. 28.

24. *The Milwaukee Journal,* December 21, 1932.

25. *Evening Independent,* February 14, 1933.

26. There has long been some dispute as to whether Jones played from a bunker or from a sandy wasteland—but there has never been a dispute regarding the quality of the shot.

27. *The Tuscaloosa News,* February 7, 1978.

28. *The Milwaukee Journal,* April 8, 1934.

29. James Dodson, *Ben Hogan: An American Life* (London: Aurum, 2004), p. 128.

30. *The Tuscaloosa News,* February 7, 1978.

31. *The Evening Independent,* January 23, 1933.

32. *The Spokesman Review,* April 6, 1933.

33. *The Milwaukee Journal,* July 23, 1933.

34. *The Youngstown Vindicator,* July 23, 1933.

35. *The Vancouver Sun,* August 14, 1933.

36. *The Deseret News,* June 29, 1933.

37. *The Palm Beach Daily News,* March 26, 1934.

38. *St. Petersburg Times,* February 28, 1933.

39. *The Tuscaloosa News,* March 9, 1934.

40. *The Reading Eagle,* April 2, 1934.

41. R.T. Jones, *Golf Is My Game* (New York: Doubleday, 1960), p. 200.

42. *The American Golfer,* September 1935.

43. *Time Magazine,* September 12, 1932.

44. *Time Magazine,* June 18, 1934.

45. *Golf Illustrated,* July 1934, p. 11.

46. Club historian, Wilshire Country Club.

47. *Golf Illustrated,* September 1934, p. 11.

48. *Ibid.,* p. 10.

49. *Ibid.*

50. *Ibid.,* p. 11.

51. *The Evening Independent,* July 18, 1934.

52. Al Barkow, *Getting' to the Dance Floor* (Springfield, NJ: Burford Books, 1986), pp. 24–25.

53. Ben Hogan, *Power Golf* (London: Nicholas Kaye, 1949), p. vi.

54. Jones, p. 92.

55. *The American Golfer,* May 1935.

56. It is well known that Jones preferred "Bob" to "Bobby," but Keeler's report referred to him as "Bobby."

57. *The American Golfer,* May 1935.

58. *Ibid.*

59. *Ibid.*

60. *Ibid.*

61. *The American Golfer,* July 1935.

62. Wind, p. 271.

63. *The Painsville Telegraph,* June 10, 1935.

64. *Ibid.*

65. *New York Times,* January 2, 1933.

66. *Golfing,* April 1936.

67. *The Daily Oklahoman,* October 24, 1935.

68. *The Glasgow Herald,* January 8, 1935.

Chapter 4

1. Barkow, *Getting' to the Dance Floor,* p. 8.

2. *Ibid.*, p. 9.

3. *The Washington Post,* September 11, 1936.

4. *Ibid.*

5. *The Pittsburgh Post-Gazette,* August 7, 1933.

6. *The Lodi Sentinel,* November 9, 1934.

7. *The Milwaukee Journal,* April 2, 1938.

8. *The Leader Post,* January 10, 1940.

9. Moss, p. 91.

10. Letter from James Tufts to Mrs. Cullum, New York, October 27, 1936, Tufts Archives, Pinehurst, NC.

11. Wind, p. 232.

12. *The American Golfer,* October 1935.

13. *Ibid.*

14. These had been approved by the USGA in 1924 and by the R&A in 1930. However, even in the United States, steel was not regularly used or indeed widely manufactured until the 1930s.

15. *The Daily Telegraph,* July 12, 2008.

16. *The New York Times,* October 11, 1930.

17. *The Milwaukee Journal,* November 22, 1936.

18. *The Milwaukee Journal,* November 19, 1936.

19. *The Milwaukee Journal,* June 6, 1936.

20. *The Calgary Daily Herald,* June 8, 1936.

21. Barkow, *Getting' to the Dance Floor,* p. 107.

22. Club historian, Salem Country Club.

23. *The Seattle Post-Intelligencer,* July 1936.

24. Nelson, p. 61.

25. *PGA Magazine,* September 1936.

26. *Ibid.*

27. *Ibid.*

28. Sam Snead, *The Education of a Golfer* (New York: Simon & Schuster, 1962), p. 35.

29. *The Eugene Register-Guard,* January 18, 1977.

30. *The Evening Independent,* January 1937.

31. Anecdote provided by Gordon McInnes, head professional at Lookout Point and whose father caddied for "Dutch" Harrison at the General Brock Open—and then went on to become head pro at the club.

32. Snead, p. 191.

33. *The Bulletin,* April 5, 1937.

34. Nelson, p. 66.

35. *Ibid.*, p. 89.

36. T. Flaherty, *The U.S. Open 1895–1965* (New York: E.P. Dutton, 1996), p. 100.

37. *Ibid.*

38. *The Evening Independent,* July 22, 1937.

39. *The Evening Independent,* April 4, 1937.

40. *The Telegraph Herald,* September 1, 1938.

41. *The Washington Reporter,* July 13, 1938.

42. *The Atlanta Constitution,* June 13, 1937.

43. *The Chicago Tribune,* November 4, 1967.

44. *The Chicago Tribune,* June 13, 1937.

45. *Ibid.*

46. *Ibid.*

47. *Ibid.*

48. *The New York Times*, June 13, 1937.

49. *The Windsor Daily Star*, September 14, 1936.

50. *The Milwaukee Sentinel*, January 11, 1926.

51. Club historian, Glen Oak Country Club.

52. Barkow, *Gettin' to the Dance Floor*, p. 30.

53. *The Reading Eagle*, July 22, 1937.

54. Nelson, pp. 76–77.

55. *The Evening Independent*, July 22, 1937.

56. *Ibid.*

57. *The Glasgow Herald*, December 14, 1937.

58. *The Reading Eagle*, July 10, 1937.

59. *St. Petersburg Times*, July 14, 1937.

60. *St. Joseph News Press*, July 13, 1937.

61. *Ibid.*

62. *The Los Angeles Times*, January 11, 1938.

63. *The Evening Independent*, August 15, 1938.

64. *The Milwaukee Journal*, April 5, 1938.

65. *Ibid.*

66. *Ibid.*

67. Flaherty, p. 100.

68. *The Sunday Morning Star*, June 5, 1938.

69. *The Pittsburgh Press*, June 8, 1938.

70. C. Fountain, *Sports Writer* (New York: Oxford University Press, 1993), p. 160.

71. *The Reading Eagle*, March 4, 1942.

72. *The Atlanta Constitution*, June 12, 1938.

73. *Ibid.*

74. *The Prescott Evening Courier*, February 2, 1940.

75. *The Middlesboro Daily News*, July 16, 1939.

76. *The Milwaukee Journal*, January 26, 1939.

77. Dodson, p. 131.

78. *The New York Times*, January 16, 1939.

79. *The Pueblo Indicator*, March 11, 1939.

80. There is no evidence that there were tax breaks for the Dapper Dan group, but in his excellent *The Golden Era of Golf,* Al Barkow refers to how, in 1932, Henry Doherty of the Miami Biltmore Hotel solved some tax problems with his staging of a golf tournament. See pp. 59–60.

81. *The Pittsburgh Post-Gazette,* May 25, 1939.

82. *The Pittsburgh Press,* June 29, 1938.

83. *The Prescott Evening Courier*, September 6, 1934.

84. *The American Golfer*, Vol. 38, 1935.

85. *The Vancouver Sun*, February 10, 1939.

86. *The Pittsburgh Press*, August 13, 1939.

87. *Ibid.*

88. Snead, p. 161.

89. *The Calgary Herald*, June 14, 1939.

90. *The Reading Eagle*, June 13, 1939.

91. *The Professional Golfer of America*, May 1939.

92. *The Milwaukee Journal*, May 2, 1939.

93. *The Telegraph Herald*, July 15, 1939.

94. *The Glasgow Herald*, February 3, 1939.

95. *The Spokesman Review*, August 27, 1940.

96. *The Milwaukee Journal*, April 24, 1940.

97. Dodson, p. 307.

98. *The Miami News*, January 3, 1940.

99. J. Burke, *It's Only a Game* (London: Penguin, 2006), p. 109.

100. *The Youngstown Vindicator*, June 10, 1940.

101. *The Telegraph Herald,* June 10, 1940.

102. *The St. Petersburg Times*, December 17, 1940.

103. *The St. Petersburg Times*, December 15, 1940.

104. *The Calgary Herald*, December 17, 1940.

105. *The St. Petersburg Times*, April 13, 1940.

106. Jones, p. 22.

107. *The Spokane Chronicle*, September 21, 1937.

Epilogue

1. *Time Magazine,* December 14, 1942.

2. *The Telegraph Herald*, June 22, 1942.

3. *The St. Petersburg Times*, December 1, 1942.

4. *The Times Daily*, April 7, 1942.

5. *The Evening Independent,* September 11, 1944.

6. *The Spokane Daily Chronicle*, February 24, 1944.

7. *The St. Joseph News-Press*, August 12, 1944.

8. Club historian, Wilshire Country Club.

9. *The Eugene Register Guard*, March 31, 1941.

10. *The Tuscaloosa News,* June 20, 1941.

Bibliography

Books

Badger, A.J. *FDR: The First Hundred Days.* New York: Hill & Wang, 1988.

Barkow, A. *Gettin' to the Dance Floor.* Springfield, NJ: Burford Books, 1986.

_____. *The Golden Era of Golf.* New York: St. Martin's Press, 2000.

_____. *Golf's Golden Grind.* New York: Harcourt Brace Jovanovich, 1974.

Benton, M. *The Velvet Touch.* Detroit: Ann Arbor Press, 1965.

Burke, J., Jr. *It's Only a Game.* New York: Gotham Books, 2006.

Corcoran, F. *Unplayable Lies.* New York: Duell, Sloan & Pearce, 1964.

Corcoran, J. *Fred Corcoran: The Man Who Sold Golf.* New York: Gray, 2010.

Cronin, T.W. *The Spirit of Medinah.* Medinah, IL: Medinah Country Club, 2001.

Degler, C.N. *Out of Our Past.* New York: Harper Colophon, 1970.

Dodson, J. *American Triumvirate.* New York: Alfred A. Knopf, 2012.

_____. *Ben Hogan: The Authorised Biography.* London: Aurum, 2005.

Flaherty, T. *The US Open 1895–1965.* New York: E.P. Dutton, 1966.

Fountain, C. *Sportswriter: The Life and Times of Grantland Rice.* New York: Oxford University Press, 1993.

Hogan, B. *Power Golf.* London: Transworld, 1963.

Jenkins, R. *Franklin Delano Roosevelt.* London: Pan Books, 2005.

Jones, R.T. *Golf Is My Game.* New York: Doubleday, 1960.

Kirsch, G. *Golf in America.* Urbana: University of Illinois Press, 2009.

Klein, B.S. *Discovering Donald Ross.* New York: John Wiley & Sons, 2001.

Lowe, S.R. *Sir Walter and Mr. Jones.* Chelsea, MI: Sleeping Bear Press, 2000

Moss, R.J. *Eden in the Pines.* Southern Pines, NC: Pilot, 2005.

_____. *Golf and the American Country Club.* Urbana: University of Illinois Press, 2001.

Nelson, B. *How I Played the Game.* New York: Dell, 1993.

Penna, T. *My Wonderful World of Golf.* New York: Centaur House, 1965.

Sarazen, G., and H.W. Wind. *Thirty Years of Championship Golf.* London: A&C Black, 1990.

Snead, S. *The Education of a Golfer.* New York: Simon & Schuster, 1962.

Tindall, G.B., and D. Shi. *America: A Narrative History.* New York: W.W. Norton, 1993.

Trebus, R.S., and C. Wolffe, Jr. *Baltusrol: 100 Years.* Lynchburg, VA: Progress Printing, 1995.

Wind, H.W. *The Story of American Golf.* New York: Alfred A. Knopf, 1975.

Newspapers

The Atlanta Constitution
The Berkley Daily Gazette
The Bulletin
The Calgary Herald
The Chicago Tribune
The Courier
The Daily Oklahoman
The Daily Telegraph
The Deseret News
The Eugene Register Guard
The Evening Independent
The Glasgow Herald
The Kentucky New Era
The Leader Post
The Lewiston Daily Sun
The Lodi Sentinel
The Los Angeles Times
The Miami News
The Middlesboro Daily News
The Milwaukee Journal
The Milwaukee Sentinel
The New York Times
The News & Courier
The Painsville Telegraph
The Palm Beach Post
The Pittsburgh Post-Gazette
The Pittsburgh Press
The Prescott Evening Courier
The Providence News
The Pueblo Indicator
The Reading Eagle
The Rochester Evening Journal
The St. Joseph News Press
The St. Petersburg Times
The Seattle Post-Intelligencer
The Spokane Chronicle
The Spokesman Review

The Schenectady Gazette
The Sunday Morning Star
The Sydney Morning News
The Telegraph Herald
The Times Daily
The Toledo News-Bee
The Tuscaloosa News
The Vancouver Sun
The Washington Post
The Washington Reporter
The Westchester Journal News
The Windsor Daily Star
The Youngstown Vindicator

Journals and Magazines

The American Golfer
Golf Digest
Golf Illustrated
Golfdom
Golfing
North American Society for Sport History: Proceedings and Newsletter
PGA Magazine
Time Magazine

Miscellaneous

Club historian, Glen Oak Country Club
Club historian, Inglewood Country Club
Club historian, Salem Country Club
Club historian, Wilshire Country Club
The Presidential Papers of Franklin D. Roosevelt
Letters from Tufts Archives, Pinehurst, NC

Index

189